	Trainer	TR/D.1	Develop applicat…
		TR/D.2	Manage the unle…
		TR/D.3	Answer the "WII…
		TR/D.4	Provide realistic…
		TR/D.5	Provide visualiza…
		TR/D.6	Give individuali…
		TR/D.7	Provide job performance aids.
		TR/D.8	Provide "Ideas and Applications" notebooks.
		TR/D.9	Create opportunities for support groups.
		TR/D.10	Help trainees prepare group action plans.
		TR/D.11	Have trainees create individual action plans.
		TR/D.12	Design and conduct relapse prevention sessions. (See Chapter 8)
		TR/D.13	Help trainees negotiate a contract for change with their supervisors.
	Trainee	TE/D.1	Link with a buddy.
		TE/D.2	Maintain an "Ideas and Applications" notebook.
		TE/D.3	Participate actively.
		TE/D.4	Form support groups.
		TE/D.5	Plan for applications.
		TE/D.6	Anticipate relapse.
		TE/D.7	Create behavioral contracts.
Following	Manager	M/F.1	Plan trainees' reentry.
		M/F.2	Psychologically support transfer.
		M/F.3	Provide a "reality check."
		M/F.4	Provide opportunities to practice new skills.
		M/F.5	Have trainees participate in transfer-related decisions.
		M/F.6	Reduce job pressures initially.
		M/F.7	Debrief the trainer.
		M/F.8	Give positive reinforcement.
		M/F.9	Provide role models.
		M/F.10	Schedule trainee briefings for co-workers.
		M/F.11	Set mutual expectations for improvement.
		M/F.12	Arrange practice (refresher) sessions.
		M/F.13	Provide and support the use of job aids.
		M/F.14	Support trainee reunions.
		M/F.15	Publicize successes.
		M/F.16	Give promotional preference.
	Trainer	TR/F.1	Apply the Pygmalion Effect.
		TR/F.2	Provide follow-up support.
		TR/F.3	Conduct evaluation surveys and provide feedback.
		TR/F.4	Develop and administer recognition systems.
		TR/F.5	Provide refresher/problem-solving sessions.
	Trainee	TE/F.1	Practice self-management.
		TE/F.2	Review training content and learned skills.
		TE/F.3	Develop a mentoring relationship.
		TE/F.4	Maintain contact with training buddies.

TRANSFER OF TRAINING

DR. MARY L. BROAD, *Defense Information Systems Agency, Washington, DC*

DR. JOHN W. NEWSTROM, *University of Minnesota, Duluth, Minnesota*

TRANSFER OF TRAINING

ACTION-PACKED STRATEGIES TO ENSURE HIGH PAYOFF FROM TRAINING INVESTMENTS

ADDISON-WESLEY PUBLISHING COMPANY, INC.

Reading, Massachusetts • Menlo Park, California • New York
Don Mills, Ontario • Wokingham, England • Amsterdam
Bonn • Paris • Milan • Madrid • Sydney • Singapore
Tokyo • Seoul • Taipei • Mexico City • San Juan

The publisher offers discounts on this book when ordered in quantity for special sales. For more information please contact:

> Corporate & Professional Publishing Group
> Addison-Wesley Publishing Company
> One Jacob Way
> Reading, Massachusetts 01867

Library of Congress Cataloging-in-Publication Data
Broad, Mary L.
    Transfer of training : action-packed strategies to ensure high payoff from training investments / Mary L. Broad and John W. Newstrom.
        p.   cm.
    Includes bibliographical references and index.
    ISBN 0-201-19274-8
    1. Employees—Training of.   2. Transfer of training.   I. Newstrom, John W. II. Title.
HF5549.5 T7N48   1992
658.3′ 12404--dc20
                                                                      91-28966
                                                                          CIP

Cover design by James F. Brisson
Text design by Wilson Graphics and Design (Kenneth J. Wilson)
Set in 10 point Palatino by Shepard Poorman Communications Corporation

ISBN 0-201-19274-8

Printed on recycled and acid-free paper.
3 4 5 6 7 8 9 -MA-96959493
Third printing April 1993

DEDICATION

This book is dedicated to our many friends and colleagues in human resource development. We thank them for their generous support, intellectual stimulation, presence, wisdom, insight, and suggestions as we prepared this book. Most of all, we thank them for their caring responses at various points in our careers whenever we needed them—and sometimes even when we didn't realize the need.

CONTENTS

Preface

Transfer of Training is based on three major premises:

(1) U.S. organizations spend billions of dollars each year on human resource development (HRD) for their employees.

(2) Most of that investment in organizational training and development is wasted because most of the knowledge and skills gained in training (well over 80%, by some estimates) is not fully applied by those employees on the job.

(3) For these organizations to remain competitive in the global marketplace, and to develop the highly skilled workforce that can contribute to solutions for the world's pressing problems, *improving transfer of training* must become HRD's top priority. Our multibillion-dollar training industry has to show that HRD investments pay off in improved performance on the job.

As we developed this book, we have constantly been enriched and challenged by the real-world practitioners who have developed and applied creative strategies to improve the transfer of training to the workplace. They are from many parts of the world: the United States, Canada, Great Britain, Europe, Latin America, Australia, and Singapore. They operate in many settings: public and private sectors, large and small organizations, management and technical training programs. These colleagues are the sources from which many of the transfer strategies in this book are drawn.

Our contribution has been to identify important concepts and strategies, refine and adapt them, sort them into meaningful categories, research key issues, develop systems and management guidelines, and test approaches in many different organizational and cultural settings. We have been amazed—and exhilarated—at the strength of positive responses from these clients and colleagues as they recognized straightforward, structured steps to accomplish the results they have struggled to obtain.

The major purpose of *Transfer of Training* is to help managers, supervisors, and all employees in any organization achieve full performance on the job. The effective transfer to the workplace of knowledge and skills learned in training is essential to support and maintain that performance.

A related, equally significant purpose for *Transfer of Training* is to elevate the role and status of the HRD function in the organization. Traditionally HRD professionals have felt "buried" several layers down on the organization chart, often in the personnel function, with little direct access to top decision makers. We describe a new role for HRD professionals—that of *manager of transfer of training*—which provides a way to position the HRD function in the strategic planning processes of the organization.

In presenting our concepts we focus on the partnership with managers and employees in organizations which is essential in effective analysis and planning for training. However, we do not address the technologies of effective *design* and *delivery* of training; these are well covered by many outstanding authors in the field.

We present key themes at the beginning of each chapter and highlight the introduction of special terms. You may either proceed through the chapters in sequence or focus on specific sections of greater immediate interest. Regardless of your method, this book establishes transfer of training as an emerging critical HRD issue and shows how you can become an effective manager of transfer for the organization(s) you serve.

We have divided this book into four sections. Part I lays the groundwork for addressing the transfer of training. Chapter 1 describes the impact of inadequate transfer and identifies the emerging role of HRD as a strategic force contributing to organizational success. It proposes an important new role for the HRD professional. Chapter 2 discusses important transfer-related research, identifies barriers inhibiting transfer, analyzes their timing and cause, and considers an application of *force field analysis*. In Chapter 3 we describe the expertise and processes necessary to move into the role of manager of transfer for the organization and then present two conditions for effective transfer: first, responsibility for improving transfer of training must be shared by managers and trainees, as well as trainers; second, the trainer plays a key role as manager/coordinator/stimulator/monitor of the entire transfer process. Chapter 4 presents the Transfer Matrix, with key roles and times to support transfer. This matrix helps you recognize the interactions among the three major role players in guiding transfer and the three key periods in which they can act.

Part II describes in detail the major transfer strategies and their applications. Chapter 5 presents strategies before training begins; Chapter 6 gives strategies during training; and Chapter 7 describes strategies after training is completed. In Chapter 8 we present the *relapse prevention* process, to build strong support for transfer into the training program.

Part III describes how to apply transfer principles and strategies in the real world of organizational life. Chapter 9 presents two examples of systematic support for transfer, and Chapter 10 provides detailed guidelines for developing and maintaining that support.

Part IV presents five useful additions to the book. Appendix A is a concise listing of all the transfer strategies discussed previously. Appendix B describes seven underlying behavioral processes that help to explain why transfer strategies work. Appendix C suggests that organizations audit both current and potential transfer support. Appendix D defines key terms used in the book, and Appendix E presents an extensive bibliography of published materials on the topic of transfer of training.

Action-oriented readers may be inclined to ask a question (posed by a well-known series of TV commercials in the 1980s), "Where's the beef?" The overly simplified answer might be that our "beef" is in Chapters 5, 6, 7, and 8, in which we describe a range of strategies to support transfer. However, we urge you to take the time to absorb the foundation material that puts our "beef" into perspective: Chapters 1 through 4 provide the critical context of challenges and needs in contemporary organizations. Similarly, Chapters 9 and 10 challenge you to develop the organizational support that is essential for effective management of transfer of training.

Acknowledgments

We are grateful to all whose work is captured, directly or indirectly, in this book. In particular, we gratefully acknowledge the ideas and support of key contributors: Robert Marx, for concepts and guidelines on relapse prevention; members of the Transfer of Training Network—especially Richard Fleming, Ray Noe, Debra Cohen, Ken Wexley, Dennis Laker, and Nevin Trammell—who provided input and feedback on various portions of the manuscript; members of the Washington HRD Consortium (particularly Maggie Bedrosian, James Jones, Linda Morris, and Carlene Reinhart) for encouragement and unflinchingly honest critiques of the entire manuscript; and Kate Habib, our supportive editor. Constructive feedback from several additional manuscript reviewers (Roxanna Fredrickson, Julie Hile, Edward W. Jones, and Edward Scannell) was invaluable in improving the quality of the final product.

Finally, we would not have reached our goal without the patience and support of Stuart Broad and Diane Newstrom. By putting up with our mental and physical absences and handling many of life's major and minor distractions, they made possible our concentrated attention to this project over many months. They deserve to be considered major contributors as well.

Mary L. Broad
Chevy Chase, Maryland

John W. Newstrom
Duluth, Minnesota

Part I
LAYING THE GROUNDWORK

Chapter 1

HRD AND THE TRANSFER PROBLEM

The successful firm in the 1990's and beyond . . . will be . . . a user of highly trained, flexible people as the principal means of adding value.
— Tom Peters, *Thriving on Chaos*

KEY THEMES FOR THIS CHAPTER:

- Human resource development (HRD): a critical resource for organizational success

- Enormous annual HRD investments, largely wasted because of inadequate transfer of training

- The Transfer Partnership: managers, trainers, and trainees

- The HRD professional: manager of transfer for the organization

HUMAN RESOURCE DEVELOPMENT: RESOURCE FOR ORGANIZATIONAL SUCCESS

As human resource development (HRD) professionals, we are proud of our contributions to the development of the nation's—and the world's—workforce. Our challenges and opportunities are escalating as a productive workforce is recognized as the primary critical resource for organizations of all kinds.

- William Johnston and Arnold Packer's landmark study, *Workforce 2000*, points out: "the foundation of national wealth is really people—the human capital represented by their knowledge, skills, organizations, and motivations. . . . Education and training are the primary systems by which the human capital of a nation is preserved and increased" (1987, 116).

3

- Tom Peters, in *Thriving on Chaos*, recommends: "Workforce training and constant retraining . . . must climb to the top of the agenda of the individual firm and the nation. Value added will increasingly come through people, for the winners. Only highly skilled—that is, trained and continuously retrained—people will be able to add value" (1988, 322).

- W. Edwards Deming, the pioneer in Total Quality Management (TQM), emphasizes the central role of large and continuing investments in training throughout his discussion of his Fourteen Points for managers in *Out of the Crisis* (1988).

With this recognition comes the challenge to develop, maintain, update, and fully apply the skills our organizations need to survive and flourish. In this book our focus is on training the workforce and on transfer of training as the ultimate payoff for the organization's investment in training.

Three fundamental concepts underlie our work: *human resource development (HRD)*, *training*, and the *trainer*.

HUMAN RESOURCE DEVELOPMENT (HRD)

HRD is the profession that helps organizations to enhance workforce effectiveness and productivity through learning and other performance improvement activities.

The clients of HRD professionals are key organizational stakeholders: executives, managers, supervisors, and all other employees. Clients may also include shareholders, customers, suppliers, and community groups.

HRD professionals support performance improvement in the organization in several ways. First, they help to identify requirements for performance improvement. These requirements might be for new skills arising from new technologies, products, or services or for improvement of skills used in current jobs. The requirements may also result from a changing work environment: the introduction of Total Quality Management, for example, or an increasingly multicultural workforce.

HRD professionals then analyze and propose changes in the work environment to support improved performance. Changes may include restructuring jobs and/or work procedures, providing specific and timely performance feedback, or revising formal or informal incentives. These nontraining interventions have only recently become widely recognized as HRD tools. Joe Harless (1970), Thomas Gilbert (1978), Robert Mager and Peter Pipe (1970), and Geary Rummler (1976) led the way in identifying the complexity of factors affecting human performance and useful strategies to improve that performance.

TRAINING

The most commonly recognized HRD strategy to improve performance, for which most organizations make most of their HRD investments, is *training*.

> *Training* consists of instructional experiences provided primarily by employers for employees, designed to develop new skills and knowledge that are expected to be applied immediately upon (or within a short time after) arrival on or return to the job.

Usually training of employees in necessary job skills is provided by employers. Occasionally potential employees are given training by the organization or by third parties such as vocational schools or adult education programs. In these cases the employee does not begin the job until after successful completion of training.

We will emphasize throughout this book that training should be undertaken only after thorough organizational and performance analyses have been done and other performance improvement interventions have been explored. These are discussed in Chapter 3. Training is expensive to design and deliver; it should be the *last*, not the *first*, intervention the HRD professional and the organization should consider in order to improve employee performance. (This principle may be difficult to maintain in the real world, where HRD professionals seldom have the luxury to follow ideal procedures. However, even if some training is mandated, it might be accompanied by improved work procedures, feedback systems, or other interventions.)

THE TRAINER

> *Trainers* are HRD professionals who analyze performance problems and design, deliver, evaluate, manage, and/or support training in a variety of ways.

This is a commonly accepted definition in many organizations. Throughout this book we will use *trainer* as a synonym for *HRD professional*: those with responsibilities for training and other HRD functions.

MASSIVE HRD INVESTMENTS

How much do organizations spend for training and other HRD activities? Anthony Carnevale and Leila Gainer estimate that U.S. employers, both public and private, spend close to $30 billion annually on *direct* costs of formal training (design and delivery of training and job-related tuition reimbursement).

This does not include *indirect* costs such as trainee salaries and costs of training facilities. In addition, U.S. employers spend between $90 and $180 billion on less-structured informal training (1989, 15). These authors estimate the total U.S. workforce at close to 120 million (p. 23).

For discussion purposes, we will conservatively estimate that at least $50 billion in both direct and indirect costs is invested annually in the United States in *formal* training (to improve employee performance in the present job). Our estimate suggests average expenditures, across the entire workforce, of more than $400 per employee per year.

Many organizations are just beginning to realize the full extent of their expenditures for training and other HRD-related activities. In the past they have considered these as expenses or costs of doing business, rather than as investments to improve productivity. Also, many organizations have traditionally looked at training or education as employee benefits without direct bottom-line impact. Recognition of HRD as a high priority worthy of significant financial support has brought new visibility for HRD as a strategic organizational investment.

These key concepts—increased priority for HRD activities and recognition of the huge investments today's organizations make in HRD—lead directly to the question: *Do organizations receive a good return on their HRD investments?* Let's take a look at what is known about those returns.

TRANSFER OF TRAINING: THE REAL PAYOFF FOR HRD INVESTMENTS

TRANSFER OF TRAINING DEFINED

Do organizations get full value for their investments in training? That is, is the training they pay for fully transferred to the job? This brings us to a very important definition.

> *Transfer of training* is the effective and continuing application, by trainees to their jobs, of the knowledge and skills gained in training—both on and off the job.

This means that trainees apply all they learned in training to their jobs, at least as well as they could demonstrate those skills at the end of the training program. Full transfer of training also means that with practice on the job, the level of skill with which that learning is applied will increase beyond the level demonstrated at the end of the training period.

THE TRANSFER PROBLEM

Is transfer of training a problem? A recent comprehensive survey of research and literature on transfer by Timothy Baldwin and Kevin Ford found the following:

> There is growing recognition of a "transfer problem" in organizational training today. It is estimated that while American industries annually spend up to $100 billion on training and development, not more than 10% of these expenditures actually result in transfer to the job. . . . Researchers have similarly concluded that much of the training conducted in organizations fails to transfer to the work setting. (1988, 63).

In one study reviewed in the Baldwin and Ford survey, John Newstrom analyzed perceptions of HRD professionals on the transfer of content of management development programs. On the average these professionals believed that only about 40% of the content of programs they conducted was transferred to the work environment immediately after training, about 25% was still being applied six months later, and—the true bottom line—a mere 15% was still being used at the end of a year. Similarly, Frank M. Hoffman (1983) reported estimates that only 10% of expenditures for training resulted in observable behavior change on the job.

It would no doubt have been in the interest of the HRD professionals who provided these estimates to be able to report higher percentages of transfer of skills to the job. They certainly would prefer to show management a much greater payoff for HRD activities. Their candor strengthens the impact of their conclusions: most training investments do not produce full and sustained transfer of new knowledge and skills to the job.

Although concern about transfer of training has grown enormously during recent years, the transfer problem has been addressed for more than 30 years. In 1955, Edwin Fleishman, Edwin Harris, and Harold Burtt conducted one of the first formal research studies relating to transfer. They measured changes in behavior of International Harvester foremen who were trained in leadership principles and techniques. Immediately following training, the foremen generally showed the desired changes in behavior. However, after some time back on the job, most had returned to their original behavior. The desired results of the training were achieved only among those foremen whose supervisors themselves consistently demonstrated the desired principles and techniques.

In one of the earliest discussions on the subject, James Mosel (1957) pointed to "mounting evidence that shows that very often the training makes little or no difference in job behavior" (p. 56). He identified three necessary conditions for transfer: training content must be applicable to the job, the trainee must learn the content, and the trainee must be motivated to change job behavior to apply what was learned. The last condition is the most difficult, Mosel stated, because it requires "rewards and punishments, incentives and deterrents *in the job situation*" (p. 57, emphasis in the original) to support transfer, and these are under *management's*—not the trainer's—control.

Others have focused on problems of transfer since the Mosel study. For example, in 1971 Leonard Nadler discussed "support systems," management actions to support transfer, organized into categories relating to level of management and timing of actions. In 1977 Training House identified 12 factors inhibiting transfer and suggested several ways to avoid or minimize each factor. In 1982 Mary Broad presented research identifying 74 actions managers can take to support transfer in several time categories. (See the bibliography in Appendix E for other references.)

Other writers have discussed one or another aspect of transfer problems. Figure 1.1 illustrates a typical transfer situation. Generally trainers put all their efforts into the needs analysis, design, and delivery of training. Research and expert professional opinion maintain that these efforts result in a relatively low level of what we might call "voluntary" or unsupported transfer. Figure 1.2 shows the goal of this book: to encourage an additional level of effort on transfer management which can result in a large increase in "stimulated" transfer.

Our experience with many organizations has uncovered a wide range of difficulties in achieving transfer of training. We have not yet found a training situation in which no transfer problems occur. In a bank operations center, for example, on-the-job training on check-processing equipment had significant gaps in transfer and maintenance of key skills. (Some transfer problems may be significantly decreased as certain skills-oriented training becomes embedded in the work itself. However, embedded training must be carefully

Figure 1.1   **LIMITED TRANSFER OF TRAINING FOLLOWING UNSUPPORTED TRAINING ANALYSIS, DESIGN, AND DELIVERY EFFORTS**

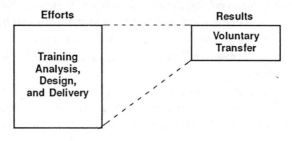

Figure 1.2 **ENHANCED TRANSFER OF TRAINING FOLLOWING TRANSFER MANAGEMENT EFFORTS**

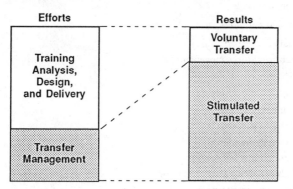

designed and tested, with attention to worker skills, communication styles, attitudes, cultures, and work site conditions.) The many training situations we have studied vary greatly in the number and complexity of transfer problems they present.

For some types of training in technical skills with clearly defined procedures, the job situation itself supports immediate transfer. The secretary must use new word-processing skills promptly on return to the job, and the quality of performance is obvious. The assembly line worker must use new statistical skills almost immediately, and correct or incorrect performance shows up right away. In these situations transfer problems can be identified promptly and appropriate corrective actions taken quickly.

However, in other technical skill situations, transfer problems are not immediately recognized or effectively addressed. The secretary's supervisor may discover repeated errors but may not know what corrective action to take. A technician may make mistakes in calculations which are not found promptly or which cannot be traced to a particular person or work site. If the problems are not constructively and promptly addressed, errors become habits and desired new skills deteriorate.

For other types of training in complex, less clearly defined skills—for example, management decision making or interpersonal communications—the opportunity to apply new skills may not arise immediately, and the job situation often does not provide direct support for transfer of those skills. Transfer problems may not be identified easily, and corrective actions may never be taken in an organized way. Employees may avoid using new skills they find difficult, or they may give up easily if they run into problems.

Table 1.1 TRAINEE/WORK CHARACTERISTICS ASSOCIATED WITH TRANSFER

1. Trainee characteristics

   A. Ability and aptitudes

   B. Personality
      (1) High need for achievement
      (2) Internal locus of control

   C. Motivation
      (1) Trainee confidence
      (2) Desire to succeed
      (3) Optional attendance
      (4) High job involvement
      (5) High belief in value of training
      (6) High self-expectancies

2. Work environment characteristics

   A. Supportive organizational climate
   B. Precourse discussion with boss
   C. Opportunity to use knowledge and skills
   D. Posttraining goal setting and feedback

Adapted from Baldwin and Ford (1988).

Factors external to the work site may also present problems for effective transfer of new skills. A reorganization may be so distracting that employees fall back on old habits without trying new behaviors. The organizational culture may discourage risk-taking behavior; trainees may be reluctant to try newly learned skills because they fear negative consequences for failure.

In their review of the literature on transfer of training, Baldwin and Ford developed categories of trainee and work environment characteristics which may support transfer of training (Table 1.1). Although definitive research is lacking, some experts suggest that trainees may be more likely to transfer new skills to the job if they have abilities and aptitudes for the new skills, personality traits such as high achievement needs and internal locus of control ("self-starters"), and motivation to use the new skills on the job.

These characteristics will not surprise experienced trainers. Trainees who are strong in these traits are often more likely to transfer new skills to the job in spite of barriers in the work environment. The problem, of course, is that trainers usually cannot select trainees according to strength in these traits. Most trainers must train those whom the organization selects, however weak the trainees may be in characteristics that support transfer.

The work environment characteristics identified by Baldwin and Ford offer more hope. These are a supportive organizational climate, precourse discussion between trainee and boss about the training, opportunity to use new
knowledge and skills on return to the job, and posttraining goal setting and
feedback from the supervisor. These are included in the many support strategies—by the manager, trainer, and trainee before, during, and after training—which we discuss in detail in Chapters 5 through 8.

Baldwin and Ford illustrated five common types of transfer situations
(Figure 1.3). In Types A, B, and C, the posttraining level of performance is
significantly higher than the pretraining level; in Types D and E, the

Figure 1.3 TYPES OF TRANSFER MAINTENANCE CURVES

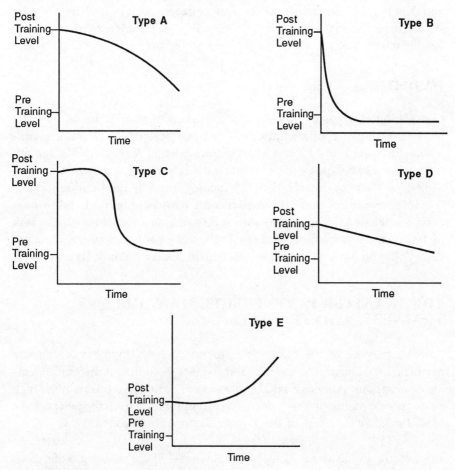

Source: Baldwin and Ford (1988). Used by permission.

posttraining level is moderately higher. However, as time goes by on the job, the level of performance in each situation begins to change.

In A, barriers to transfer (to be discussed in Chapter 2) are strong, transferred skills are gradually abandoned, and performance approaches the pretraining level. In B, barriers are insurmountable, application of new skills drops precipitously, and performance decreases below the pretraining level. In C, barriers seem to be eliminated and application of new skills improves, then something happens, and performance of new skills drops to the pretraining level. In D, barriers prevail and the low posttraining level of performance of new skills drops steadily to the pretraining level.

Type E shows a much more successful outcome. Posttraining skill levels may be low, as shown, or high. Back on the job, over time and presumably with frequent practice and support, the level of performance is maintained and then improves as trainees become more experienced in applying the new skills. This is the goal we all hope to attain, in which barriers to transfer have been eliminated or controlled so that new skills can be used and improved.

WASTED HRD INVESTMENTS

Considering all types of training and low levels of transfer found by HRD researchers, a generous assumption is that perhaps 50% of all training content is still being applied a year after training delivery. Considering our rough estimate of $50 billion spent on formal training per year, that means a *loss of $25 billion a year* to organizations for training not fully used on the job.

Trainers must be proactive in addressing barriers to transfer and managing a coordinated, organization-wide approach to finding solutions. The lack of full transfer of training requires a comprehensive response, pulling together all who have an impact on the organization's training activities.

THE TRANSFER PARTNERSHIP: MANAGERS, TRAINERS, AND TRAINEES

A major purpose of this book is to promote the development of effective partnerships of *managers*, *trainers*, and *trainees* to address transfer problems in organizations. Although HRD professionals (whom we call trainers) may be our primary audience, we address transfer problems from the perspectives of all three key members of the *Transfer Partnership* (see Figure 1.4).

Trainees are the learners—usually employees—whose training, education, and development are sponsored by the organization to improve organi-

Figure 1.4   THE TRANSFER PARTNERSHIP

Trainee:
Recognizes need
for new skills

Trainer:
Designs and/or delivers
learning experiences

Trainee

Manager:
Supports learning
and application
on the job

Trainer

Trainee

Illustration by Tom Broad

zational functioning and productivity. The trainee recognizes needs for new skills.

Trainers include all HRD-related professionals; they may be internal consultants (employees of the organization) or external consultants who assist organizations on a temporary basis. The trainer manages the design and/or delivery of learning experiences.

Managers include all in the organization with authority and responsibility for accomplishing an objective or mission through the efforts of others, from the chief executive officer (CEO) to the first-line supervisor and team or group leader. The manager supports learning and application on the job.

The *Transfer Partnership* is made up of managers (including executives, supervisors, team leaders, etc.), trainers, and trainees who have a strong interest in a particular training program and who have agreed to work together to support the full application of the training to the job.

We propose that a Transfer Partnership be formed for every high-priority training program; Chapter 10 discusses this process in detail. The training program that the Transfer Partnership supports may be short (a day or less) or long (a series of events stretching over months or years). The training may be in the classroom, individualized, or embedded in the work itself. Managers may serve in the trainer role for some or all of the training. The only true requirement for a Transfer Partnership is for all partners—managers, trainers, and trainees—to be committed to making the training investment pay off.

Trainers have long been key players in developing the organization's employees. Managers have started to take a more active role in developing their subordinates. Currently organizations are beginning to recognize that trainees are not passive onlookers in the HRD enterprise. The complex knowledge and skills needed by employees to function effectively are constantly growing. Trainees must be encouraged to take greater responsibility for their own development of new knowledge, skills, and abilities; they are vitally important members of the Transfer Partnership.

Each partner has an important contribution, and full transfer requires that all partners cooperate to maximize the application of new knowledge and skills to the job. Together their partnership in planning and implementing transfer strategies—before, during, and after training—will bring a highly leveraged payoff of enhanced transfer for all the organization's training efforts. In Chapters 5–8 we explore in detail the many strategies each partner can use to support more effective transfer of training.

The trainer's role, however, is pivotal to produce the transfer payoff. Trainers now have an important new role: to help the other partners—and the organization—recognize and address the training transfer problem.

NEW HRD ROLE: MANAGER OF TRANSFER OF TRAINING

As the HRD field has evolved, trainers and other HRD professionals have often taken new roles. Primarily classroom instructors at one time, they are now being asked to provide expertise in analysis, design, use of media, evaluation, group facilitation, management of the HRD function, and other special skills.

The new organizational spotlight on HRD as a strategic investment opens up a new and highly visible role, that of *manager of transfer of training* for the organization. This role has three important responsibilities: developing the Transfer Partnership for each high-priority training program, managing all Transfer Partnerships, and serving as advocate for transfer in the organization. This new role is discussed in detail in Chapter 3.

The new role of manager of transfer brings trainers several benefits and one major challenge. The benefits for trainers, internal or external, are greater visibility, leverage, and a strategic role in the organization's functions. The challenge is that trainers must be prepared to demonstrate state-of-the-art HRD expertise—not only in current HRD activities but also in new approaches and technologies to meet new requirements. Trainers must be able to show that HRD investments pay off in improved job performance, increased productivity, and greater contributions to all stakeholders. A strong focus on transfer of training is the key to that payoff.

Trainers are starting to move into the role of manager of transfer of training. They care deeply about the issue of transfer because it affects their roles and status in their organizations. Trainers (and this includes all HRD professionals) have, or can develop, the expertise to be manager of transfer for their organizations. This book is designed to help them do just that.

In forward-looking organizations, managers recognize the clear need for effective training that is fully applied on the job; they will welcome all constructive initiatives. The success of the organization depends in large part on effective transfer of employee training to the work site—and trainers are the experts who can help make transfer happen.

Trainers are also beginning to contribute to the strategic planning process in progressive organizations, applying their special skills to developing and maintaining an effective workforce. HRD is increasingly seen as a strategically essential function for improving both productivity and quality of work life in our organizations. The trainer, as manager and advocate for transfer, is key to the organization's continuing success.

References

Baldwin, Timothy T., and Kevin J. Ford. "Transfer of Training: A Review and Directions for Future Research." *Personnel Psychology* 41 (1988): 63–105.

Broad, Mary L. "Management Actions to Support Transfer of Training." *Training and Development Journal* (May 1982): 124–30.

Carnevale, Anthony P., and Leila J. Gainer. *The Learning Enterprise*. Alexandria, Va.: American Society for Training and Development and the U.S. Department of Labor, Employment and Training Administration, 1989.

Deming, W. Edwards. *Out of the Crisis*. Cambridge: Massachusetts Institute of Technology, 1988.

Fleishman, Edwin A., Edwin F. Harris, and Harold E. Burtt. *Leadership and Supervision in Industry*. Monograph no. 33. Columbus: Personnel Research Board, Ohio State University, 1955.

Gilbert, Thomas F. *Human Competence: Engineering Worthy Performance*. New York: McGraw-Hill, 1978.

Harless, Joe E. *An Ounce of Analysis Is Worth a Pound of Objectives*. Newnan, Ga.: Guild V Publications, 1970.

Hoffman, Frank O. "Is Management Development Doing the Job?" *Training and Development Journal* (January 1983): 34–39.

Johnston, William B., and Arnold H. Packer. *Workforce 2000: Work and Workers for the 21st Century*. Indianapolis: Hudson Institute, 1987.

Mager, Robert F., and Peter Pipe. *Analyzing Performance Problems, or "You Really Oughta Wanna."* Belmont, Calif.: Fearon Publishers, 1970.

Mosel, James N. "Why Training Programs Fail to Carry Over." *Personnel* 34, no. 3 (1957): 56–64.

Nadler, Leonard. "Support Systems for Training." *Training and Development Journal* (October 1971): 2–7.

Newstrom, John W. "Leveraging Management Development through the Management of Transfer." *Journal of Management Development* 5, no. 5 (1985): 33–44.

Peters, Tom. *Thriving in Chaos: Handbook for a Management Revolution*. New York: Alfred A. Knopf, 1988.

Rummler, Geary A. "How to Determine What Problems Can—and Can't—Be Resolved by Training." *Training* 13, no. 8 (August 1976): 18–21.

Training House. *Reasons Why Training Programs Succeed or Fail*. Princeton Junction, N.J.: Author, 1977.

Chapter 2

BARRIERS TO TRANSFER OF TRAINING

Training can only elaborate on that which already exists; it cannot create new behavior for an environment that will not support it.
— Alex Mironoff, "Teaching Johnny to Manage"

KEY THEMES FOR THIS CHAPTER:

- Perceptions of executives and trainers
- Timing of barriers
- Responsibility for barriers
- Lewin's change model and force field analysis

DEFINING THE TRANSFER PROBLEM

Assume that you, as manager of HRD for your organization, have decided to address a performance problem that has training implications. This problem has become obvious as a result of a recent study evaluating the results of training efforts. You wish to find out why the training you oversee—both in-house and off site, on-the-job and off-the-job, managerial and job skill, short term and long term—does not pay off consistently in measurable results.

The implications of your analysis are clear: a problem exists somewhere in the overall training process. Unless it can be identified and resolved, organizational support (both philosophical and financial) for future centrally managed human resource development efforts will be dramatically reduced. The HRD function in your organization is a profit center (for example, you receive revenues from the line units for the estimated overall costs of training each employee they send to you). However, your department's profits will fall below acceptable levels unless line managers can be convinced that there is a substantial payoff from training for their departments.

You begin by developing a tentative definition of the apparent problem to guide your thoughts: "The organizational investment in training does not currently pay off in behavioral change and organizationally useful results." You then convert the problem statement into two questions for exploration: "Why *doesn't* training transfer to the workplace? What are the barriers that keep trainees from fully applying newly learned behaviors to their jobs?" One fruitful place to begin the search for an answer to this question is a review of what is currently known about actual and potential transfer barriers in other organizations. This chapter will do that for you.

BARRIERS TO TRANSFER

Very little empirical research on transfer barriers has been conducted and reported. Two relevant studies, both dealing with perceptions, will be summarized here. Each provides some important clues for further in-house exploration.

PERCEPTIONS OF EXECUTIVES

A survey of top executives by John Kotter (1988) reported four major factors that frequently inhibited the success of training and development efforts to improve the performance of managers. The most powerful of these inhibiting forces was a lack of involvement by top management in the behavior change process (reported by 71% of the respondents). A second factor was the recognition by 51% of the respondents that new efforts to improve were too centralized in the top echelons of the organization, resulting in little acceptance by lower-level participants. Third, new efforts to improve employee behavior were believed by 21% of the executives to be too staff centered, with insufficient participation by the direct users. Finally, 17% of the executives believed that expectations from the training programs were often unrealistic: too much was expected too soon. In addition, a broad range of programs and practices affecting employee development were assessed by 57–93% of respondents as being less than adequate to support the need for spotting high-potential supervisory personnel, identifying their developmental needs, and then meeting those needs.

Kotter's findings suggest that barriers to transfer of all types of training may occur relatively often in organizations (especially at higher levels) and that those barriers represent substantial impediments to change. Kotter concluded that *"many* firms have *many* practices that are less than adequate to

Table 2.1 TRAINERS' PERCEPTIONS OF BARRIERS TO TRANSFER

Rank Order	Barrier
1	Lack of reinforcement on the job
2	Interference from immediate (work) environment
3	Nonsupportive organizational culture
4	Trainees' perception of impractical training programs
5	Trainees' perception of irrelevant training content
6	Trainees' discomfort with change and associated effort
7	Separation from inspiration or support of the trainer
8	Trainees' perception of poorly designed/delivered training
9	Pressure from peers to resist changes

Key: 1 = greatest barrier; 9 = lowest barrier

support the need to attract, retain, develop, and motivate a sufficient leadership capacity in management (1988, 113).

PERCEPTIONS OF TRAINERS

In another investigation, Newstrom studied transfer barriers in two stages (1986). First, a group of 24 trainers identified the major impediments to the successful transfer of training in their organizations. Their responses were classified into nine distinct categories. From this a second questionnaire was constructed and administered to a set of 31 trainers from a diverse range of organizations. They were instructed to rank order the nine categories of barriers according to their perception of the relative influence against transfer (1 = greatest barrier; 9 = lowest barrier). Their responses were tabulated, averaged, and used to create an overall rank-ordered list of the most potent impediments to transfer of training. Table 2.1 presents the results of that study.

The most significant barrier, in the eyes of trainers, is the *lack of reinforcement on the job* to support trainees in applying training to their jobs. In effect the trainers were saying, "Trainees don't expend the energy to do something new because no one around them seems to care." This dramatic perception, of course, sharply contradicts what is widely known about how people best learn and retain information, as well as how they can be motivated on their jobs.

The second most powerful impediment to transfer reported by Newstrom is interference by the immediate environment (work and time pressures, insufficient authority, ineffective work processes, inadequate equipment or facilities) with transfer of knowledge and skills to the workplace. This implies that even if trainees are willing to change, they still cannot use their new skills because of obstacles (real or imagined) placed in their way—a powerful barrier.

The third most important barrier is lack of active support by the organizational climate (culture) for the transfer of the program's content or skills to the workplace. This is consistent with the lack of specific reinforcement for behavior change, but on a much broader scale. The trainers polled believed that the typical organization simply doesn't provide strong philosophical support for the goals of training and development programs.

Several other impediments received relatively high rankings: trainees' belief that training programs are impractical or irrelevant to their needs and that proposed changes would cause them undue discomfort or extra effort. Lower-ranked barriers include the loss of motivation when trainees are separated from the inspirational presence of the trainer, perceptions that training programs were poorly designed or delivered, and pressure on trainees by their peers not to transfer training to the workplace (e.g., "Don't rock the boat for the rest of us"). Unsolicited responses provided additional speculative reasons for poor transfer, including trainee fear of failure, deeply ingrained resistance to any change, mandated attendance (many trainees do not feel a need for the training), lack of authority to implement desired changes, long elapsed time before opportunities arose to try applying learned skills, and incompatibility of material with trainees' values and beliefs.

BARRIERS TO TRANSFER

Problems can usually be solved more easily if they are well defined and classified for easy identification. The same is true of barriers to transfer. We have examined the major impediments to transfer of training and classified them along two dimensions that we believe are important and useful to trainers. First, when do the impediments usually arise? Second, which source or role is primarily responsible for the impediment?

TIMING

Table 2.2 shows the results of our first analysis. We classified each of the nine major barriers to transfer into the most likely (indicated by 1), and the second most likely (indicated by 2) *time* period in which that barrier would arise:

Table 2.2 TIMING OF BARRIERS TO TRANSFER

Dominant Timing			Barrier
Before	During	After	
		1	Lack of reinforcement on the job
	2	1	Interference from immediate (work) environment
1	2	2	Nonsupportive organizational culture
	1		Trainees' perception of impractical training programs
	1		Trainees' perception of irrelevant training content
2	2	1	Trainees' discomfort with change and associated effort
		1	Separation from inspiration or support of the trainer
	1		Trainees' perception of poorly designed/delivered training
2		1	Pressure from peers to resist changes

Key: 1 = primary time of impact; 2 = secondary time of impact

before, during, or after training occurs. This reveals several interesting phenomena and results in several conclusions.

First, the barriers are, to some degree, a problem *throughout* the three major time periods affecting the training process. Nevertheless, the majority of 1's appear in the "After" column, indicating the distinctive presence of negative threats to transfer during that time period.

Second, barriers are a more frequent problem during the training program and after the training program than before training. On the positive side, these high-barrier periods are fruitful times for improving the transfer-of-training process.

Third, the barriers are most dominant after the program is formally over (five factors have primary impact, and one has secondary impact). This is consistent with the widespread and erroneous perception that transfer of training needs attention only after training has been completed. The number of barriers with primary and secondary impact before and during training shows that attention must be given in these time frames as well.

Fourth, four barriers appear in *two or more* time periods. Therefore, if these barriers could be diminished or removed, the overall transfer process would be improved during more than one time period.

A simple but powerful conclusion emerging from our analysis of the timing of barriers is that an *organization cannot wait until after a training program is over to address the transfer-of-training problem.* Barriers to transfer of

Table 2.3 SOURCE OF BARRIERS TO TRANSFER

| Dominant Sources | | | | Barrier |
Trainee	Trainer	Manager	Organization	
2		1	2	Lack of reinforcement on the job
		2	1	Interference from immediate (work) environment
			1	Nonsupportive organizational culture
2	1	2		Trainees' perception of impractical training programs
2	1	2		Trainees' perception of irrelevant training content
1	2			Trainee discomfort with change and associated effort
2	2	1		Separation from the inspiration or support of the trainer
2	1	2	2	Trainees' perception of poorly designed/ delivered training
		2	1	Pressure from peers to resist changes

Key: 1 = primary responsibility; 2 = secondary responsibility

training should be eliminated or reduced before, during, and after training. In Table 2.2 we indicate when various barriers will most likely affect transfer, thus allowing trainers and managers to focus their analytical and problem-solving efforts.

SOURCES

A similar analysis of the primary *responsibility* (e.g., source of control, or cause) for impediments to transfer is shown in Table 2.3. Here we have identified the four primary sources of responsibility: the trainees themselves, the trainer, the direct manager of the trainee, and the organization in general (such as top management, the trainee's peer group, and physical factors in the work environment). Again, our assessment of both primary and secondary responsibility for the impediments is shown. Some interesting conclusions emerge.

First, managers hold the most significant keys to resolving the problem of transfer of training. Not only are they a secondary source for five of the nine factors, but they hold the primary responsibility for the number one overall impediment: *absence of reinforcement on the job for the newly acquired skills and abilities.* At least in the eyes of organizational trainers, uninvolved managers who fail to support and encourage the application of learning on the job represent the major barrier to transfer, and hence they are a primary target for change. (Managers also need to address and compensate for the lessened motivation for transfer that may result when trainees become separated from inspirational trainers following a training program.)

Second, trainers hold primary responsibility for any problems concerning training that is impractical, irrelevant, or poorly designed or delivered. Although trainers can't totally *control* trainee perceptions of these factors, trainers' decisions can clearly affect them. As we pointed out in our discussion of managerial responsibilities, these trainee perceptions are likely the result of trainers who are not in touch with managers and trainees on felt needs, priorities, organizational directions, operating problems, and so on.

Certainly if the trainee's perceptions (for example, that the training is impractical) are valid, then the trainers must assume primary responsibility. Although this shared responsibility (between reality and trainee perceptions) in no way absolves trainers from taking greater control over transfer of training, it does indicate that the basic problem may be complex. Trainers also have secondary responsibility, with trainees and/or managers, for trainee discomfort with change and for the loss of motivation associated with separation from the trainer following training. Again, trainers can influence managers to support this continued contact.

Finally, the sources of several major barriers are partially within the trainees themselves. At least three may be *perceptual* (but nevertheless very real): trainee beliefs that the training is impractical, irrelevant, or poorly designed or delivered. Trainees also are a primary barrier source due to their own attitudes regarding the personal costs (discomfort, increased effort) associated with change. In addition, trainees may be a secondary barrier source if they are "seduced" into unquestioning acceptance of training content while in the presence of a skillful, expert, or inspirational trainer, only to discover that the "spell" wears off upon returning to work. We suggest that trainees need to share some of the responsibility for differentiating between useful new knowledge and skills and the motivational impact of the trainer's presence.

Other barriers throughout the organization also result in the limited impact of contemporary training programs. These include the absence of a strong organizational culture specifically supporting training and its applications, physical obstacles to transfer, and peer group pressures that tell recently trained employees not to change their practices. The organization in general has primary responsibility for these barriers, which can also interfere with transfer of the best-intended training.

UNDERSTANDING BARRIERS

In this section we review the change process as it affects common barriers to effective transfer of training. Here we present some of the potential problems inherent in gathering data on stakeholders' perceptions of transfer problems. We believe you will benefit greatly from examining the wider context of individual and organizational behavior provided here. It will help you to become more sophisticated at identifying and fine-tuning the most appropriate actions to support transfer in your organization.

A CHANGE MODEL

Kurt Lewin, a pioneering social psychologist, believed that complex problems should be viewed in elementary ways (1951). He contended that sophisticated and complex models may obstruct our thinking. By contrast, a rich potential, and even an inherent elegance, exists in simpler views of reality. This "simpler model" approach helps to sort out the most important elements in a situation and to aid in discovering the fundamental relationships among them. Further, Lewin suggested that it was useful to borrow and apply relevant conceptual models from other fields to stimulate new thinking and shed light on current problems.

Lewin believed that a change in any existing social system (or set of behaviors) could best be viewed and managed as a three-step process: *unfreezing, change,* and *refreezing* (see Figure 2.1). Lewin's change model has been widely applied since he introduced it more than 40 years ago; it is frequently used in organizational development programs as a fundamental framework or paradigm. We will explain it briefly and illustrate the potential application of Lewin's concepts and recommendations to the design and implementation of a transfer program.

Figure 2.1 LEWIN'S CHANGE MODEL

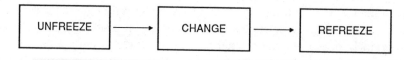

Unfreezing

The first step in Lewin's change process is unfreezing. First, he suggested, trainers should direct their energies toward the prerequisites to change. The trainer as change agent must recognize that the path must be cleared to make it possible even to consider—much less to embrace—change. People have acquired many attitudes, values, and habits over time; these will likely interfere with the acquisition of new learning unless dealt with first. Consequently, Lewin recommended that trainers and other change agents support the process of unfreezing an old behavior from someone's repertoire before considering how to instill a new one.

Unless the unfreezing step is consciously considered, the training task will be like trying to force liquid into a bottle that is already full. The same problem occurs in an intellectual sense with training: pouring new knowledge into an already filled (or closed) mind is not likely to be productive, nor will it produce lasting effects. Minds are usually not like clean slates (unlike the myth of *tabula rasa*) but contain much information and many experiences. (For example, simply telling people the health risks associated with smoking has not always been highly effective in changing their behavior.)

Fortunately, several ideas exist for facilitating the unfreezing/unlearning process. For example, trainees can be encouraged to let go of old habits and practices through a variety of unlearning tactics (Newstrom, 1983). They can be induced to make public announcements of their intentions to change, and they can identify intrinsic and extrinsic rewards to be gained for doing so. Peer pressure and social rewards from others for dropping old habits can be invoked, and overpowering feedback can be provided.

Other unlearning tactics include the simple passage of time to aid forgetting, total immersion in a new activity to capitalize on the distraction effect, invoking the fear of failure from continued pursuit of old behaviors, or even erecting direct physical barriers to prevent the recurrence of previous practices.

Change

Lewin next turned his attention to the change process itself. He suggested that the relative ease of inducing a new behavior is the product of the interplay between two opposing sets of forces. In effect, every system (or person) can be viewed as either being in equilibrium or seeking it. Equilibrium is a steady-state balance between the opposing forces that drive toward behavioral change and those that restrain it. Because change represents a disruption of equilibrium, it requires an upset in the existing "field" of forces to bring it

Figure 2.2 FORCE FIELD ANALYSIS

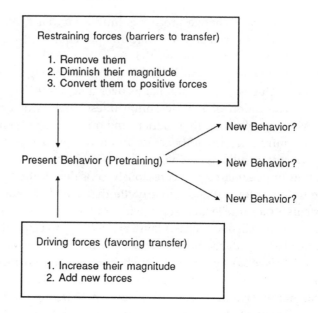

about. This process of analyzing the factors working for (driving forces) and against (restraining forces) change is called *force field analysis* (see Figure 2.2).

For example, a brusque and insensitive customer service representative can be considered to be in equilibrium between forces driving toward change (e.g., desire for approval from one's supervisor; awareness of customer preferences for high-quality treatment) and forces restraining change (e.g., deeply ingrained habits; social approval from peers). For change to occur (long-term continuous improvements in service quality), the balance of these factors must favor the driving forces.

Driving forces. Trainers should consider one or both of the following approaches to adjusting the driving forces that encourage trainees to change:

(1) Identify the existing set of driving forces for change, and try to increase the *magnitude* of one or more of those for an overall net gain in the desired direction.

(2) Add new positive incentives to those already being used.

Restraining forces. It is also possible to induce behavioral change by reducing or eliminating the set of forces that currently act to restrain change.

This is the primary focus of this chapter; elimination of barriers has, in our experience, a quick and often dramatic effect on increasing transfer of training. Three alternatives exist: (1) Trainers and managers can examine a restraining force that inhibits change and try to *remove* it; (2) they can attempt to *diminish* the impact of any one restraining force; or (3) they can unleash their own creativity by actually trying to *convert* restraining forces into driving forces.

The five tactics for bringing about change—by adjusting driving forces and/or reducing or eliminating restraining forces—are illustrated in Figure 2.2.

Refreezing

The third phase in the overall change process is called *refreezing*. Lewin recognized that there is a fundamental and dramatic difference between knowing what to do differently (as a result of training, for example), and actually doing it on the job. For effectiveness, newly acquired skills must be converted into habits that become used almost unconsciously. New habits are best solidified through regular practice opportunities and extensive reinforcement of the acquired skills.

RELATING FORCE FIELD ANALYSIS TO BARRIERS TO TRANSFER

We have isolated three different phases in the training process and targeted different strategies for each one. We can also view a trainee as a system of forces in a temporary state of equilibrium (within larger organizational systems, of course). Planned change can be consciously induced by upsetting that equilibrium through *ethical* manipulation of the restraining and driving forces.

In this spirit, we view manipulation as the examination and control of key variables surrounding the employee so as to induce and maintain desirable behaviors. The goals are legitimate within the organization, and both cues and reward systems can be made known to the employee. Therefore, "manipulation" is not an attempt to convert employees into something they don't want to be or will not personally gain from. It is done only with the best interests of both parties in mind.

Our experience with transfer-of-training problems in organizations leads us to believe that restraining forces should be examined first. Elimination or reduction of these forces is often easier and faster than trying to develop and install competing driving forces. So, following Lewin's lead, we generally recommend looking at the specific factors that serve as barriers to transfer of training within organizations.

SUMMARY

Barriers to transfer of training exist in all organizations to varying degrees. Returning to the example at the beginning of this chapter, we suggest that you, as manager of HRD, search for the major in-house barriers unique to your situation. The data and conclusions presented here should provide strong clues about where to look, but other barriers may be found as well. A fruitful data-gathering process would entail a survey of key stakeholders to elicit their perceptions of actual transfer barriers. The information obtained would provide a strong foundation for preparing an action plan to overcome such barriers.

When we suggest strategies for preventing and overcoming barriers to transfer of training in Chapters 5, 6, 7, and 8, we will continue to focus on the three periods of the training cycle: before, during, and after training. We will also focus on the three major areas of responsibility for barriers to transfer: the trainer, the trainee, and the manager/organization. These two broad factors—timing and responsibility—provide the best approach for most trainers to analyze barriers in the organizations they serve.

We also applied Kurt Lewin's widely accepted change model to the barriers to transfer that exist in organizations today. We believe that the probability of transfer in any organization can be dramatically increased if the forces *for* change are increased and if the forces *against* change are diminished or removed.

References

Kotter, John P, *The Leadership Factor*. New York: Free Press, 1988.

Lewin, Kurt. *Field Theory in Social Science*. New York: Harper and Row, 1951.

Mironoff, Alex. "Teaching Johnny to Manage." *Training* (March 1988): 53.

Newstrom, John W. "The Management of Unlearning: Exploding the 'Clean Slate' Fallacy." *Training and Development Journal* (August 1983): 36–39.

———. "Leveraging Management Development through the Management of Transfer." *Journal of Management Development* 5, no. 5 (1986): 33–45.

Chapter 3

MANAGING TRANSFER OF TRAINING

A clearly defined system should be initiated which unites the trainer, trainee, and the manager, where possible, in the transfer process.
— Melissa Leifer and John Newstrom, "Solving the Transfer of Training Problems"

KEY THEMES FOR THIS CHAPTER:

- The HRD function linked to the organization's strategic direction
  —Shared decision making by managers and trainers
  —Seven key decisions on performance improvement
- The trainer's recognized expertise
  —State-of-the-art knowledge and skills in HRD
  —Consultant skills
- The trainer's primary role as manager of transfer of training

Ensuring effective transfer of training so that the organization's HRD investment pays off is not a simple matter. There are many specific small-scale strategies for managers, trainers, and trainees; these are presented in Chapter 5–8. Their full and continuing effectiveness depends on two HRD roles for the trainer: being seen as a strategic organizational resource, and being recognized as an HRD expert and skilled consultant. With these supporting roles in place, the trainer can move into the primary role of *manager of transfer* for the organization. This chapter addresses these important roles and the expertise they require.

LINKING THE HRD FUNCTION TO THE ORGANIZATION'S STRATEGIC DIRECTION

Strategic planning is an essential process in today's organizations. The HRD function has an important role as a *strategic resource* in that process.

Strategic planning is a formal organizational process that develops a shared set of beliefs about the organization's desired future and goals and identifies the functions, priorities, and resources that are necessary to reach those goals.

As Neal Chalofsky and Carlene Reinhart (1988) emphasize, linkage of all HRD activities to the organization's strategic direction is essential. Trainers must be part of the strategic planning process and give expert advice on workforce development implications. They must be fluent in the organization's jargon—needs, goals, priorities, plans, operations, people, and culture—as well as the industry of which it is a part, to be accepted as a full partner with top decision makers.

To align HRD efforts with the organization's strategic goals, trainers must share decision making with management, particularly in making key decisions on performance improvement.

DECISION-MAKING MODELS

In Chapter 1 we proposed a Transfer Partnership among managers, trainers, and trainees to ensure that training investments pay off through full transfer of training to the job. Because managers and trainers have the earliest and most important roles in key decisions about training, we will look first at their involvement in making those decisions. The trainee's role becomes more important at later stages in the performance improvement process.

In contemporary organizations, decisions about performance improvement in general—and training in particular—are made in many ways. We have simplified these into three basic models, graphically shown in Figure 3.1:

(A) decisions primarily by managers (or other organizational leaders),

(B) decisions primarily by trainers, and

(C) decisions shared by managers (or other organizational leaders) and trainers.

As we discuss the models, we encourage you to determine the level of involvement of managers and trainers in key decisions in the organizations you serve. That level of involvement may lie at any point on the continuum shown in Figure 3.1.

DECISIONS PRIMARILY BY MANAGERS

In the 1920s and '30s, before training became a recognized field, major decisions about training were made almost exclusively by managers or other organizational leaders who claimed no training expertise (A in Figure 3.1). Generally there was a full supply of workers, and job tasks were not complex; organizations could usually hire people with the skills they needed rather than train their employees.

After World War II, many organizations developed internal training staffs. These were often "subject-matter experts" in knowledge or skills important to the organization. Training still was not widely recognized as a specialty, and managers continued to make most training-related decisions.

In spite of the growing expertise of many trainers, this model of training decisions primarily by managers (or other organizational leaders) is still common in many organizations. These managers identify training needs and support training activities. The trainer responds to management's requests, administers the training function, and may deliver training as well.

DECISIONS PRIMARILY BY TRAINERS

In the 1940s and '50s, a body of knowledge began to develop concerning the complex factors affecting human behavior and the systems and procedures that are necessary to produce constructive and long-lasting behavioral change. Leonard and Zeace Nadler (1989) identified the *laboratory method, human relations training,* and *programmed instruction* as significant early trends. The American Society for Training and Development (ASTD) was formed in 1942. University graduate programs began to appear in adult education and, later, in human resource development.

As training expertise became recognized, some organizations gave responsibility for training decisions to the training staff. This model of training decisions primarily by trainers (B in Figure 3.1) is common in many organiza-

Figure 3.1   LEVELS OF INVOLVEMENT IN TRAINING-RELATED DECISIONS BY MANAGER AND TRAINER

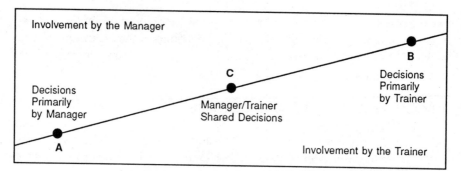

tions today. These trainers identify and provide training they think the organization needs without much interaction with managers.

COMMON ASSUMPTIONS IN BOTH MODELS

Both models—decisions primarily by managers or primarily by trainers—remain common patterns of responsibility for training in many organizations. Unfortunately, both models have failed to produce fully effective transfer of training to the job because both are based on similar false assumptions:

- Most performance problems can be solved by training.

- The training function in an organization is primarily administrative, not a strategically important resource for the organization.

- Managers and trainers can operate without substantive interaction.

As a result, the organization's training is vulnerable to all barriers to transfer which we presented in Chapter 2. Let's look at what often happens.

IMPACT OF MANAGERS' OR TRAINERS' DECISIONS ON BARRIERS TO TRANSFER OF TRAINING

To illustrate these models, here are two hypothetical examples; they are typical alternative scenarios involving training for customer service representatives at the Ace Products Corporation. Ace customer service "reps" handle all contacts with customers primarily by phone. These include price and product inquiries, sales, shipping arrangements, and complaints.

Scenario A (decisions primarily by managers): Top Ace Products managers decide that the reps need a refresher course on customer service skills. They reached this conclusion by noting that sales figures had leveled off compared with regular increases in previous years. The managers ask the Ace Corp. trainer to arrange customer service training for the reps.

Scenario B (decisions primarily by trainers): The Ace trainer receives a brochure in the mail from XYZ Associates announcing a two-day course entitled "New Trends in Customer Service." The trainer decides it is time for more customer service training, as a number of new employees have come into that job since the last in-house training.

Both scenarios: The Ace trainer contacts XYZ Associates. Their price is right and they have good references, so the Ace trainer arranges to have XYZ deliver the training a month later. Trainees rate the course highly, Ace managers and the trainer hope that sales will improve, and all go back to business as usual.

Unfortunately, sales figures do not improve significantly. Many reps do not use the new skills. The Ace managers and trainer conclude that XYZ Associates' training was ineffective.

Let's review the major barriers to transfer of training (see Chapter 2, Table 2.1) as we look at training for Ace customer service reps. Decisions to present training were made solely by Ace *managers* (Scenario A) or by the Ace *trainer* (Scenario B) without thorough needs analyses. Important information about barriers was not discovered, basic organizational problems—for which training is *not* the solution—were not resolved, barriers to transfer of skills learned in training remain, and the training investment is wasted.

(1) *Absence of reinforcement on the job:* The immediate supervisors of the reps were not consulted by top managers (Scenario A) or the trainer (Scenario B). The supervisors think training is unnecessary because reps are already providing good customer service. Therefore, the supervisors do not reinforce the training on the job.

(2) *Interference from the immediate environment:* The reps have not received a promised on-line data base on each customer's previous orders, which would support improved customer service. They also have no time (as phones ring off the hook) to try newly learned skills.

(3) *Nonsupportive organizational climate:* New customer service techniques presented by XYZ trainers involve taking time to establish and build rapport with customers; this clashes with the Ace high-pressure climate to get to the next call as soon as possible.

(4) *Impractical training (as seen by trainees):* Although the Ace trainees enjoyed the training, they are convinced that they don't have time to apply it properly on their jobs.

(5) *Irrelevant training (as seen by trainees):* The reps do not believe they need training in customer service skills. They are sure that the on-line data base will help improve sales by making their jobs easier. They also believe the real sales problem results from rising customer complaints about durability of a major Ace product.

(6) *Trainees' discomfort with change:* Ace trainees are apprehensive about their ability to use new communication styles in the high-pressure work situation.

(7) *Separation from the trainer:* The trainees were able to learn and demonstrate new communication styles in the protected training environ-

ment, with support from the charismatic XYZ trainers. However, back on the job, they can't apply the new skills in the high-pressure work setting without additional support from those trainers.

(8) *Poor training design and/or delivery:* Practice sessions during training were limited, so trainees are not sure how to apply new skills on the job. The Ace trainer did not review the training design and materials in advance to ensure that the training followed sound principles of adult learning and instructional design.

(9) *Negative peer pressure:* Experienced Ace reps don't like the new techniques and pressure their newer co-workers to stick to the previous, less time-consuming procedures.

Any of these barriers may prevent Ace's customer service reps from applying new skills to their jobs. Although the training may be the "latest thing" in customer service techniques, it has little impact. This is too often the case when managers or trainers do not share in performance-related decisions.

DECISIONS SHARED BY MANAGERS AND TRAINERS

Today, in increasing numbers of organizations, managers and trainers share information and expertise to make informed decisions about performance improvement. This is the shared decision-making model (C) shown in Figure 3.1. Several related factors have led to this collaboration.

- Many organizations now realize that previous training investments have not paid off in transfer of skills and improved job performance.

- These organizations recognize that a skilled, flexible workforce is essential for success in today's highly competitive global economy.

- These organizations see the HRD function's direct impact on improving productivity and competitiveness and have linked it directly with formation and implementation of their strategic plans.

Examples are the organizations that have received ASTD's Corporate Awards for excellence in recent years for their strategic investments in HRD: IBM, Motorola, Dayton-Hudson, Ford, Aetna, and Xerox.

As ASTD (1988) pointed out,

Competitive companies invest in their human capital and develop it strategically. They build competitiveness out of knowledge, skills, and effort. With training and development, they link performance and commitment to a common vision of what the company intends to be.

How does investment in corporate learning pay off in the ability to make a profit, serve customers, and change to keep ahead? By linking the performance of the workforce to these competitive capabilities:

- developing a global perspective
- transforming the organization through leadership
- fostering innovation
- collaborating in nontraditional alliances
- serving the customer with quality
- producing more with less
- integrating technology and human resources
- training and developing employees continually (p. 7)

INVOLVEMENT OF EMPLOYEES IN SHARED DECISION MAKING: AN EMERGING TREND

Although managers and trainers still play the major roles, trainees have begun to bring their experience and insights to the Transfer Partnership. Employees are involved in many decisions that previously were management's alone; as Tom Peters says, "Involve all personnel at all levels in all functions in virtually everything" (1988, 284). Trainees usually become partners in the Transfer Partnership *after* initial decisions have been made, as the focus shifts to supporting full transfer of training to the job.

In organizations in which employee involvement groups are fully established, the co-workers of trainees may also participate in decisions and activities supporting performance improvement. They might be union representatives on joint labor-management committees or team members in Total Quality Management efforts. They may be experienced workers who belong to the various cultures in the increasingly diverse workforce who help managers and other workers understand those cultures and adapt work procedures accordingly. Co-workers provide information to managers, trainers, and trainees and may share in decisions by managers and trainers as well. However, we see co-workers primarily as providing support, and not as a separate partner in the Transfer Partnership.

Shared responsibility and cooperation of managers, trainers, and trainees (supported by co-workers), are essential to make effective decisions on performance improvement. Together their expertise and commitment link the HRD function to the organization's strategic direction, support greater transfer of training to the job, and make investments in training pay off. In the next section we look at the key decisions on performance improvement that managers and trainers should share.

KEY DECISIONS ON PERFORMANCE IMPROVEMENT

Over the last two decades HRD professionals have become increasingly so-phisticated at identifying important decisions that must be made to achieve improved performance. These decisions are made primarily by managers and trainers as partners, with increasing input from trainees and co-workers.

We focus on seven key decisions that lead to and follow from the decision to train. Contributors to our list include Thomas Gilbert, Joe Harless, Roger Kaufman, Robert Mager and Peter Pipe, Leonard and Zeace Nadler, Geary Rummler, and others. We add a strong emphasis on transfer of training, which most HRD experts have treated lightly or overlooked completely.

Each key decision represents many subsidiary decisions. We have not listed every step necessary for improving employee performance. (For exam-ple, Kaufman shows 10 steps in "needs analysis." We have included the en-tire process—and others—in our first key decision, identifying the need for performance improvement.) All will not agree fully with our list of key deci-sions. However, because our focus is on one essential part of the performance improvement process—managing transfer of training—we believe that this list is sufficient for examining the roles of managers and trainers in key decisions.

Key performance improvement decisions leading to and following from the decision to train should be seen as a never-ending cycle to maintain con-tinuous improvement. The seven key decisions are shown graphically in Fig-ure 3.2. (Note that decisions 5 and 6 are separated only by a dotted line; this indicates that these decisions should be worked on simultaneously.)

The key decisions, and some important considerations for each, are as follows:

(1) *Identify the need for performance improvement.* What are perfor-mance requirements? Is there a performance problem, and do we need to solve it? Is there an opportunity to improve quality of ser-vices/products?

(2) *Identify the probable causes of the performance problem/opportunity.* What are characteristics of performers and managers? Is there inter-ference from the work environment, or lack of motivation or incen-tive? Do employees need additional knowledge or skill, because of changed customer expectations or development of new technologies, processes, products, and/or services? Does a changing, culturally di-verse workforce need support in understanding, accepting, or adapt-ing new work procedures?

Figure 3.2 KEY PERFORMANCE-RELATED DECISIONS LEADING TO, AND FOLLOWING FROM, THE DECISION TO TRAIN

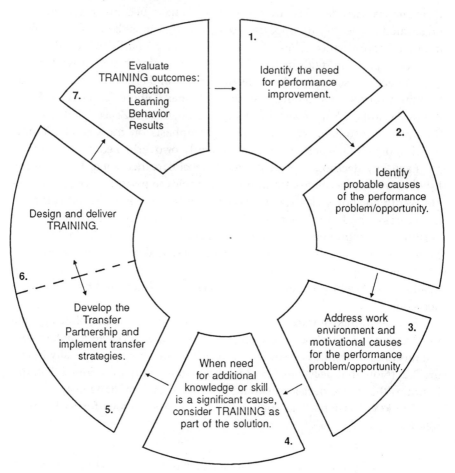

(3) *Address work environment and motivational causes for the performance problem/opportunity.* Do information flow, work procedures, equipment, reward systems, workplace learning systems, and so on, support the desired performance? Are there cultural blocks or negative consequences for the desired performance? Are there positive consequences for avoiding the desired performance?

(4) *When need for additional knowledge or skill is a significant cause of the performance problem/opportunity, consider training as part of the solu-*

tion. Could a job aid replace some or all of the training? Can training be embedded in the job? How and where should training be presented? Will relapse prevention be an important part of the training? (See Chapter 8.)

(5) *Develop the Transfer Partnership and implement transfer strategies* (in conjunction with Decision 6). What barriers interfere with transfer of training to the job? What strategies by managers, trainers, and trainees will eliminate or reduce these barriers? How will these strategies be implemented and managed?

(6) *Design and deliver training* (in conjunction with Decision 5). What are the performance objectives? What criterion tests determine if objectives are reached? What are content and prerequisites? Are all aspects of the training in line with the organization's and the workforce's cultures? Who are the participants? What resources will be allocated?

(7) *Evaluate training outcomes.* How do participants and trainers rate the training? To what extent do participants achieve the performance objectives? Do follow-up evaluations show that training was successfully transferred to the job? Have organizational products and/or services improved as a result of the training? Should the training be revised?

Evaluation results (from the seventh decision) give information on levels of performance after training. Continuing or new performance problems and/or opportunities lead again to the first decision, and so the cycle continues.

These key decisions, in order, address several major barriers to transfer. Later in this chapter we will show how shared decision making by managers and the trainer at Ace Products Corporation diminishes or eliminates these barriers.

THE TRAINER'S EXPERTISE

We have described the trainer's important supporting role as a strategic resource for management in the strategic planning process and in shared decisions on performance improvement. The trainer must also be accepted by the organization in another supporting role, as an expert HRD resource. The trainer must be recognized as an expert with state-of-the-art HRD knowledge and skills to develop cost-effective programs supporting strategic goals, and with strong consultant skills to support constructive organizational change.

STATE-OF-THE-ART EXPERTISE IN HRD

There is yet no consensus among HRD professionals on the necessary skills, knowledge, and abilities that constitute HRD expertise. Several significant recent efforts contribute toward identifying the components of that expertise. In 1986 the National Society for Performance and Instruction (NSPI) published volume 1 of the *Introduction to Performance Technology*, which focused on problem solving, analysis, nontraining solutions, and managing change. The next volume in the series will deal with instructional technology.

In 1986 the International Board of Standards for Training, Performance, and Instruction began publication of a series on competencies in HRD roles: *Instructional Development Competencies: The Standards* (1986), *Instructor Competencies: The Standards* (1988), and *Training Manager Competencies: The Standards* (1989). Future volumes will cover performance technologist and evaluator competencies.

In 1989 ASTD published *Models for HRD Practice*, with analyses of future forces affecting the HRD profession, critical HRD outputs (products or services) and quality requirements, essential competencies, and the key roles for HRD professionals.

Eventually, as the HRD profession matures, these views of the field will begin to merge. For now trainers should explore these and other models of HRD expertise and select the one most compatible with their needs and interests.

We consider it essential for every trainer/HRD professional to be in a constant learning mode, to continually enhance critical HRD competencies in our highly dynamic field. We must keep up with research and "best practices" in areas such as adult learning, needs analysis, performance analysis, instructional design, training delivery systems, motivation and reward systems, management of HRD, and evaluation. Constantly upgraded HRD expertise is necessary to earn our place as an organizational expert resource.

EXPERTISE IN CONSULTING SKILLS

Well-honed consulting skills are essential for the trainer to be effective as an HRD resource and a partner with management. As an expert consultant, the trainer supports the organization's members at all levels in working toward constructive organizational change. This may mean assisting groups in becoming effective teams, helping an executive work through a difficult reorganization decision, or supporting employee involvement groups in identifying and recommending solutions to work process problems.

Whether internal or external to the organization, the trainer must be skillful in all major phases of the consulting process. As defined by Peter Block, these phases are entry and contracting; data collection and diagnosis; feedback and the decision to act; implementation; and extension, recycle, or termination (1981). Skills in all phases are necessary to help the HRD function become recognized as a strategic resource to the organization, and to build the trainer's personal credibility as a resource for planned change.

As trainers move into the primary role of manager of transfer for the organization, they need constant updating in both supporting roles, as a strategic resource and an expert HRD resource. A personal development plan— and commitment to update and follow it constantly—are essential to develop and maintain our HRD and consulting expertise. (An example of the development process is given in Chapter 10.)

THE TRAINER AS MANAGER OF TRANSFER FOR THE ORGANIZATION

THE TRAINER'S PRIMARY ROLE

We have described two important supporting roles for the trainer. First, as a strategic resource, trainers link the HRD function with the organization's strategic goals by sharing in key performance improvement decisions. Second, as an expert HRD resource, trainers are recognized by the organization as experts in HRD technologies and best practices and in consulting skills to support organizational change.

In this section we describe the primary role that is based on these roles and is the focus of this book: *manager of transfer of training* for the organization. In this role the trainer serves as the expert and advocate to the organization for support for full transfer of training. This primary role, and its supporting roles, are shown in Figure 3.3.

It is not necessary for the trainer to achieve full success in either of the supporting roles before moving into the primary role of manager of transfer. In Figure 3.3 the dotted lines and double-pointed arrows between roles indicate that the roles interact. Developing expertise and recognition in any of the roles helps to increase expertise and recognition in the others. (This is discussed further in Chapter 10.)

As manager of transfer, the trainer works with managers at all levels (top executives, managers, supervisors, team leaders, and so on) to advocate an organization-wide focus on transfer. For each major HRD program, the

Figure 3.3   THE TRAINER'S PRIMARY ROLE AS MANAGER OF TRANSFER OF TRAINING AND SUPPORTING ROLES AS STRATEGIC AND EXPERT RESOURCE

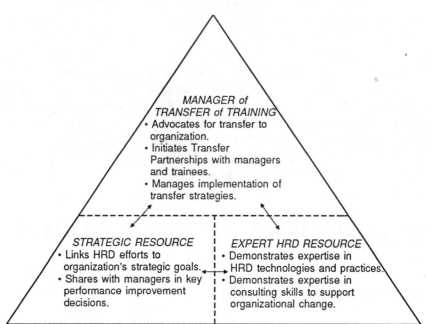

MANAGER of TRANSFER of TRAINING
- Advocates for transfer to organization.
- Initiates Transfer Partnerships with managers and trainees.
- Manages implementation of transfer strategies.

STRATEGIC RESOURCE
- Links HRD efforts to organization's strategic goals.
- Shares with managers in key performance improvement decisions.

EXPERT HRD RESOURCE
- Demonstrates expertise in HRD technologies and practices.
- Demonstrates expertise in consulting skills to support organizational change.

trainer initiates the Transfer Partnership with managers and trainees and manages the implementation of transfer strategies.

MANAGING TRANSFER AT ACE PRODUCTS CORPORATION

Let's take another look at the hypothetical example of the Ace Products Corporation to see how the trainer and managers might interact from the start as partners in working through the seven key decisions on performance improvement (Figure 3.2). In this example the trainer operates in all three roles, sharing decision making with managers, providing HRD and consulting expertise, and acting as manager and advocate for transfer.

When Ace Corp. managers discover that sales figures have not increased, they ask the trainer (and perhaps other human resource analysts) to help solve the problem. Together, they proceed through the key decisions.

(1) *Identify the need for performance improvement.* Managers and trainer look for possible causes for sales leveling off in the past year. They discover

many recent customer complaints about durability of a major product, increasing complaints from the Ace Shipping Department about shipping errors by customer service reps, and a high turnover rate among the reps. Managers and trainer agree that complaints of errors by reps suggest a need for performance improvement; they will pursue this together. Separately, managers will look into complaints about product durability, and the trainer will explore the high rep turnover rate.

(2) *Identify probable causes for the performance problem/opportunity.* The managers and trainer first interview the reps' supervisors. They find that 13 of the 30 reps joined Ace in the last three months and have never received formal training. They have had only brief coaching by rather harried supervisors, who say there has been no time for more training because the high turnover has kept them shorthanded. There has been no increase in customer service staff in the last four years, although sales volume steadily climbed during the first three of those years. The supervisors feel that significant sales opportunities are being lost because the reps don't have time to develop rapport with customers and probe for additional needs that Ace products could meet.

The trainer interviews five experienced reps who have been in their jobs more than two years. They confirm a significant workload increase and express bitterness at higher-level managers who had not kept a promise to provide a new computerized system to access information on previous customer orders. They feel the system would make their jobs easier and help to generate more sales through greater knowledge of customer needs. The reps have stayed in their jobs primarily because their supervisors are very supportive in spite of difficult work conditions. They had often reported increasing customer complaints about durability of a major Ace product but feel the reports were never read or acted upon by top managers.

The trainer tracks down seven reps who left Ace in the last few months. Two had left for non-work-related reasons. The other five all report that they left the job because of the high-pressure work situation. They also say that the number of reps had not increased for several years, though sales had been increasing until recently. Each rep had faced a significantly heavier workload without the computerized system that had been promised but never delivered.

Ace managers and trainer agree that the probable causes for the performance problems—sales and shipping errors—are:

- Lack of knowledge/skill: inadequate knowledge among new reps of Ace products and sales/shipping procedures

- Interference from the work environment: the increased workload for all reps that pressures them into choosing speed over accuracy

- Interference from the work environment, lack of motivation/incentive: lack of commitment to accuracy by the reps who feel that management had not followed through on a promise to provide the new computerized system which would make their jobs more manageable.

The managers and trainer also agree that there is an opportunity to increase sales by using the promised computerized system and by training reps (as the supervisors suggested) in more interactive but time-consuming techniques to build greater rapport with customers. This adds to the work environment problem of heavy workloads unless additional staff is added.

The managers and trainer decide that the product durability problem is not directly related to the performance problem. However, a change in materials for one component earlier in the year appears to be the cause of the durability problem; this will be pursued and solved by the managers.

(3) *Address work environment and motivational causes for the performance problem/opportunity.* The promised computer hardware is actually in the warehouse, but the Information Systems Department has not yet made a choice between two software options. The trainer also receives an analysis by the supervisors that adding four customer service rep positions would handle increased workload as well as more time-consuming interactive work processes.

The managers agree to insist—at high management levels—on an immediate decision on software. The managers and trainer agree to develop a "crash" proposal to top management to highlight the sales crisis and urge quick action. The proposal will recommend immediate purchase of the selected software and hiring of four additional customer service reps. The proposal will also show how a change to more rapport-building interactive techniques by all reps can increase sales. (The proposal includes important recommendations on training; see Decision 4.)

The managers and trainer get approval from Ace top management to expedite selection and purchase of the necessary software. They also get approval to hire four more reps and switch to new customer service techniques, with the understanding that sales will have to go up significantly by the end of the next quarter or the staff will be gradually reduced to current levels.

(4) *Where need for additional skill/knowledge is a significant cause of the performance problem/opportunity, select training as part of the solution.* The Ace trainer gains the cooperation of the Engineering and Marketing departments

in developing training recommendations. The recommendations and budget are approved by Ace top management. They are:

- The Ace trainer and Engineering/Marketing staff will present in-house training for new reps immediately on Ace products and procedures.

- The Ace trainer will identify an outside resource to train all reps (new and experienced) in rapport-building customer service techniques, linked to the new computerized system.

- The trainer will work with Engineering and Marketing to develop and train reps to use a new products and procedures handbook linked to the new computerized system and to the new customer service techniques.

- The trainer will review the training component of the new system to ensure that it is instructionally effective and adapted to reps' needs.

(5) *Develop the Transfer Partnership and implement transfer strategies* (in conjunction with Decision 6). The trainer briefs managers on Transfer Partnership concepts: barriers to transfer; key roles and times for supporting transfer; and a comprehensive list of strategies by managers, trainees, and trainers to support full transfer of training to the job. Together they select specific support strategies for managers to use. (All concepts—barriers, roles, times, and strategies—are fully explored in Chapters 4 through 8.)

Managers and the trainer identify all managers (supervisors, midlevel managers, and top executives) to participate in the Transfer Partnership. They brief these managers on the four training-related initiatives and enlist their help in selecting and participating in strategies to support transfer of training—before, during, and after training.

The reps' supervisors brief all reps on top management's support for prompt installation of the new computer system, hiring additional reps, changing to new rapport-building techniques, and developing the new products and procedures handbook. The trainer briefs the reps on the Transfer Partnership to develop support from all partners to help the reps fully transfer all new skills to the job. The reps also help to select the strategies they can use themselves to support transfer of their new skills.

The trainer schedules a series of meetings with all partners—supervisors, other managers, trainees, and the outside training consultants—before, during, and after training to ensure that all understand their roles and get the support they need to carry out all transfer strategies.

(6) *Design and deliver training* (in conjunction with Decision 5). The trainer briefs the managers on selection of XYZ Associates to deliver their highly rated program, "New Trends in Customer Service." XYZ will adapt

the program to link with the new computer system and with the planned Ace products workshops and handbook, and will provide a follow-up session one month after training to review successes and resolve problems. XYZ also recommends another consultant who has worked with them before on developing procedures handbooks tailored to the client's needs.

The trainer reports to the managers on arrangements with the Engineering and Marketing staffs to design workshop sessions on Ace products. The trainer also has reviewed the training provided by the computer system's vendor. Additional practice sessions have been included at the end of that training to be sure that trainees are comfortable with their new skills before using them on the job. Finally, the trainer shows how all components can be funded within the established budget.

The managers support the trainer's plans and arrangements. They review the transfer strategies they will take to support the various training components and proceed to carry them out with support and guidance from the trainer. XYZ Associates trainers and reps also implement their planned transfer strategies.

(7) *Evaluate training outcomes: reaction, learning, behavior, results.* The trainer briefs the managers on Donald Kirkpatrick's (1987) four levels of evaluation and describes the evaluation plans that have been prepared for each training component. The evaluations include trainee reactions, assessment of trainee learning at the end of training, supervisors' evaluations of trainees' behavior back on the job, and results—impact on sales figures, considering other factors that also affect sales. The trainer will also evaluate how effectively transfer strategies were carried out by each member of the Transfer Partnership.

The managers agree to support and participate in the evaluation process. They review the evaluation results for each level with the trainer and assess the effectiveness of the transfer strategies that were used. Overall, managers, trainer, and trainees are pleased with the high level of transfer of skills to the job. At the end of the next fiscal quarter, sales figures have increased significantly. Top management agrees to maintain the increased staffing level for customer service reps. The managers who worked with the trainer in the Transfer Partnership agree to meet regularly to monitor sales and look for other ways to provide continued support for the reps.

SUMMARY

This chapter completes the foundation and context within which we explore transfer of training in detail in the remaining chapters. We presented three important roles for the trainer. In one supporting role, as a *strategic resource,* the trainer links HRD efforts to the organization's strategic goals and shares in key decisions on performance improvement. In the other supporting role, as an *expert HRD resource,* the trainer has recognized expertise in HRD knowledge and skills, to develop effective HRD programs, and in consulting skills, to support organizational change. Finally, we explored the trainer's primary new role as *manager of transfer of training* for the organization: advocating transfer and developing and managing the Transfer Partnership.

In the next five chapters we will zero in on transfer strategies. Chapter 4 presents a simple matrix for considering *key roles and times* for supporting transfer. In Part II we explore *strategies* for managers, trainers, and trainees *before, during, and after* training. Chapter 8 describes *relapse prevention,* a special action-planning strategy for trainees returning to work environments with particularly difficult and intransigent barriers.

We encourage readers to approach these chapters from the mindset of the *manager of transfer* for the organization. In this role the trainer is highly sensitive to the issues, concerns, and pitfalls that have made problems of transfer so important for organizations today. The trainer is also the bearer of good news to the organization: many strategies have been successful in all types of organizations to eliminate barriers and support the full transfer of training to the job. We hope readers will experience many "A-ha's" in discovering transfer strategies that hold the promise of significant boosts in transfer of training for the organizations they serve.

References

American Society for Training and Development. *Gaining the Competitive Edge.* Alexandria, Va.: ASTD, 1988.

Block, Peter. *Flawless Consulting: A Guide to Getting Your Expertise Used.* Austin, Tx.: Learning Concepts, 1981.

Chalofsky, Neal E., and Carlene Reinhart. *Effective Human Resource Development: How to Build a Strong and Responsible HRD Function.* San Francisco: Jossey-Bass, 1988.

Gilbert, Thomas F. "A Question of Performance: Applying the PROBE Model (Parts I and II)." *Training and Development Journal* (September 1982): 20–30, (October 1982): 85–89.

Harless, Joe E. "Wasted Behavior: A Confession." *Training* (May 1989): 35–38.

International Board of Standards for Training, Performance, and Instruction. *Instructional Development Competencies: The Standards.* Evergreen, Colo.: Author, 1986.

———. *Instructor Competencies: The Standards.* Evergreen, Colo.: Author, 1988.

———. *Training Manager Competencies: The Standards.* Evergreen, Colo.: Author, 1989.

Kaufman, Roger. "Assessing Needs." Chapter 3 in *Introduction to Performance Technology.* Washington, D.C.: National Society for Performance and Instruction, 1986.

Kirkpatrick, Donald L. "Evaluation." In *Training and Development Handbook.* 3d ed., edited by Robert L. Craig. Sponsored by the American Society for Training and Development. New York: McGraw-Hill, 1987.

Leifer, Melissa S., and John W. Newstrom. "Solving the Transfer of Training Problems." *Training and Development Journal* (August 1980): 42–46.

Mager, Robert F. *Making Instruction Work, or Skillbloomers.* Belmont, Calif.: Lake Publishers, 1988.

Mager, Robert F., and Peter Pipe. *Analyzing Performance Problems, or "You Really Oughta Wanna."* Belmont, Calif.: Fearon Publishers, 1970.

McLagan, Patricia A. *Models for HRD Practice.* Washington, D.C.: American Society for Training and Development, 1989.

Nadler, Leonard, and Zeace Nadler. *Developing Human Resources* (3d ed.). San Francisco: Jossey-Bass, 1989.

National Society for Performance and Instruction. *Introduction to Performance Technology,* Vol. 1. Washington, D.C.: Author, 1986.

Peters, Tom. *Thriving on Chaos: A Handbook for a Management Revolution.* New York: Alfred A. Knopf, 1988.

Rummler, Geary A., and Alan P. Brache. *Improving Performance: How to Manage the White Space on the Organization Chart.* San Francisco: Jossey-Bass, 1990.

Chapter 4

THE TRANSFER MATRIX: KEY ROLES AND TIMES TO SUPPORT TRANSFER

Observe due measure, for right timing *is in all things the most important factor.*
— Hesiod, *Works and Days* (p. 694, emphasis added)

KEY THEMES FOR THIS CHAPTER:

- Identifying and classifying transfer strategies
- Key roles in support of transfer
- Critical time frames for supporting transfer
- Most potent and most frequently used role and timing combinations

This chapter will distinguish among the three major role players in the transfer process: the manager, trainer, and trainees. We also identify the three key time frames for transfer strategies: before, during, and after training. We will report the results of a study that targets the most potent and most frequently used role and timing combinations. This will set the stage for detailed discussions of a wide array of transfer strategies in the following four chapters. These transfer-related actions can aid in the process of *benchmarking*—identifying and using excellent transfer management practices by successful companies.

IDENTIFYING AND CLASSIFYING TRANSFER STRATEGIES

Over the last decade we have carefully examined extensive reports in the training literature and professional practices on the subject of transfer of training. We have read widely, attended seminars and conference presentations, corresponded with other interested practitioners and researchers, examined our own and others' organizational practices, and engaged in extensive brainstorming with selected peers. As a result, this book represents the current state of the art regarding transfer management practices.

The products of our intense interest in transfer of training have been many and diverse. First and foremost, we have been able to identify and catalogue a large number of distinct strategies that have been used by one or more organizations to facilitate transfer of training. The good news is that *a technology for transfer now exists*, even if it is still in the formative stage of development and empirical verification. This was not true only a decade ago and until now has not been available in any integrated format.

Second, we fully appreciate the difficulties often encountered by organizations, managers, supervisors, employees, and trainers in making transfer happen. It is highly frustrating when transfer doesn't occur following a successful training experience. It is even more frustrating when the trainer doesn't know why transfer did not occur. This immediately suggests that organizations need to obtain and use internal measures of the level of transfer and analyze the data to identify the most likely explanations.

Third, we soon realized the importance of creating order out of the apparent chaos surrounding the intricacies involved in transfer management. This realization ultimately led us to develop our three-stage, three-role model of the transfer process. This model will serve as the foundation for Chapters 5 through 8.

Fourth, our immersion in the field of transfer has encouraged us to search for those transfer strategies that have greater practical potential for inducing change. To find these strategies, we have surveyed several groups of trainers to tap their operating experience and perceptions. Some of the major findings will be reported here.

Finally, we fully believe that much work remains to be done on transfer management. In particular, the *quality* of research conducted to date is woefully low, as much of the emerging literature has been restricted to casual reports on single examples of organizational attempts to improve transfer. On the brighter side, the past few years have been marked by an explosion of interest in researching transfer of training. The transfer field is currently highlighted by an encouraging number of solid empirical studies and conceptual developments (see Appendix E). Collectively, these new products hold real promise of helping to build a more solid foundation for future practice.

ROLE PLAYERS

From our comprehensive review of the transfer literature emerged a simple yet useful structure for differentiating among sets of transfer strategies. As noted in Chapter 2, we quickly learned that various people and groups play roles in helping transfer take place. We found reports of peers and co-workers, supervisors, the overall organization, the trainees, the trainer, the instructional designer, and others all helping to facilitate transfer. It was clear to us that some focus was needed to make sense of that vast array of information.

Two discrete role players quickly came into view. The *trainees* are often the central figures, as they choose (consciously or unconsciously) whether to admit deficiencies, attend the training, open themselves up to new learning, make commitments to change, and carry them out. Further, they bring with them into training an array of talents, abilities, backgrounds, cultures, motivational desires, and career aspirations that need to be considered. Trainees will always be key role players in the transfer process.

Similarly, the *trainers* (whether they are program designers, external trainers, content matter specialists, or line supervisors acting as temporary trainers) can be instrumental in facilitating transfer. Beyond the obvious requirement of providing high-quality and relevant training, their influence extends in many ways to the trainees, both directly and indirectly. Unfortunately, the transfer responsibility of trainers has not always been recognized or fully accepted.

Many other factors remain: the external environment and economic conditions in particular; the organization's structure, culture, and reward system; and the peers, job supervisor, and upper management of the firm. At the risk of diminishing each factor's uniqueness, we have put all of these into a single category. Further, because we believe that management is a powerful factor in inducing or constraining change, we have labeled this category *the manager* to indicate its focal point of control. Together, these three role players—the trainee, the trainer, and the manager—constitute the Transfer Partnership. The following four chapters identify many specific strategies primarily under the control of the trainer, the trainee, and the manager.

TIME PERIODS

A second major dimension emerged clearly from our examination of the transfer literature and exploration of successful transfer practices. Some organizations were taking action only after trainees returned to their jobs; others focused on the time trainees were in the classroom itself; a few others seemed to be thinking about transfer problems long before the training began. Therefore, we adopted a three-part classification scheme that divided transfer strategies into those being initiated or taking place *before* the trainees begin training, *during* the time they are in training, and at any time *after* training is over. Although these periods remain somewhat broad, they are highly consistent with other processes within the training function, such as the classic instructional design–delivery–follow-up model.

Several other dimensions of transfer could have been used. One is the distinction between "near" and "far" transfer (Laker, 1990). *Near transfer* is the extent to which individuals apply what was acquired in training to situations very similar to those in which they were trained. The success of near transfer depends heavily on the *identical elements* approach, in which the training experience closely approximates the task demands of the job itself. *Far transfer*, by contrast, is the extent to which the trainees apply the training to novel or different situations from the ones in which they were trained. The success of far transfer often depends on the presence of general principles that trainees can acquire and apply to new and novel problems. Laker, in his model of transfer, also distinguished between transfer initiation and maintenance, thus breaking the "after" time period into a continuum from immediate to long term.

THE TRANSFER MATRIX

We combined the time dimension (before-during-after) with the *role* dimension (manager-trainer-trainee) to produce a 3 × 3 matrix of nine cells (see Figure 4.1). This is consistent with our previous analysis and classification of barriers to transfer along the same two dimensions. The results are twofold: (1) a convenient and systematic format for our presentation and discussion of a large number of transfer strategies and (2) an analytical tool for trainers to answer the contingency-oriented question "If I (or trainees, or managers) wish to intervene at any time (before, during, or after), which subset of transfer strategies should I consider?"

To fill in the matrix, we conducted an extensive and ongoing search of the training literature, focusing heavily on the past two decades. We supplemented the strategies discovered from these reports with ideas generated from our own experience. We also received direct contributions from many of our training peers, who comprise an informal network of interested research-

Figure 4.1   THE TRANSFER MATRIX: NINE POSSIBLE ROLE/TIME COMBINATIONS

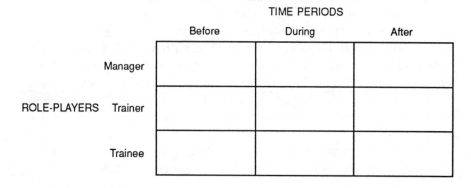

ers and practitioners. These processes resulted in a comprehensive set of 79 conceptually distinct transfer strategies.

The assignment of the individual transfer strategies to one of the nine cells was strongly substantiated by our use of a panel of experts in transfer of training. The five members of this panel were individually presented with the entire set of strategies and asked to classify each one into the appropriate category. Only those strategies with a very high degree of interrater reliability (consistent classification by 80% of the experts) were allocated to that cell and retained.

This nine-cell matrix also became the basis for gathering some data from an organizationally mixed group of trainers on their perceptions of transfer strategies. Specifically, we first asked them to report which time-role combinations of strategies they believed were *currently used most frequently* in their organizations. The rank-ordered results have been corroborated and endorsed since then by many other groups in a wide range of organizational settings, both in the United States and internationally. These results appear in Figure 4.2.

These trainers reported that they themselves made the most significant effort during training to stimulate transfer. They also felt they worked nearly as hard before training to facilitate the transfer process. The third and fourth ranks revealed their perceptions that trainees made earnest attempts to apply what they had learned by engaging in transfer actions during and after training.

The most conspicuous low ranking (9) is the frequency with which they believe managers attempt to aid the transfer process following training. Support by managers before training is also seen as relatively low (5). Clearly, in the eyes of these trainers and many others with whom we have consulted, *managers do not consistently and powerfully support the transfer of training in the work environment.* We believe that this represents a fundamental problem, and also a substantial opportunity for improvement.

Figure 4.2 PERCEPTIONS OF MOST FREQUENTLY USED ROLE/TIME COMBINATIONS FOR USING TRANSFER STRATEGIES

		TIME PERIODS		
		Before	During	After
	Manager	5	6	9
ROLE-PLAYERS	Trainer	2	1	7
	Trainee	8	3	4

Key: 1 = high; 9 = low frequency

Figure 4.3 PERCEPTIONS OF MOST POWERFUL ROLE/TIME COMBINATIONS FOR USING TRANSFER STRATEGIES

		TIME PERIODS		
		Before	During	After
	Manager	1	8	3
ROLE-PLAYERS	Trainer	2	4	9
	Trainee	7	5	6

Key: 1 = high; 9 = low frequency/potency

We next asked the trainers to assess the role-time combinations that would have the greatest impact on transfer by using the associated transfer strategies. The rank-ordered results appear in Figure 4.3. Here our question was, "Which role-time combination would produce the most powerful transfer effects, if used properly?" Here the trainers responded that transfer, to be most effective, requires managers to lay the foundation for transfer before trainees ever enter training ("manager-before" was ranked 1). This was followed by "trainer-before" (2) and then "manager-after" (3). Least powerful, they believed, was trainer follow-up after training was completed (9).

We then combined both rankings to compare the trainers' perceptions of both frequency of use and powerful potential effects for transfer strategies in each role-time combination (see Figure 4.4). We examined the result to assess current *low frequency* of use (e.g., ranks of 7, 8, or 9) and *highly powerful* effects (e.g., ranks of 1, 2, or 3). Improving the frequency of use of these particular role-time combinations would have the greatest predicted effect on improving organizational transfer of training.

We found two role-time combinations that had substantial spreads between their two rankings: "manager-before" (fifth-ranked frequency and highest-assessed potential effect) and "manager-after" (lowest-ranked frequency and third-ranked potential effect). Clearly, the manager of the trainees must become more involved in the Transfer Partnership to provide the necessary support for making transfer a reality. This involvement should be targeted at managerial strategies both before and after training occurs.

It is possible that the trainers we surveyed were biased in their perceptions and responses. They may have unfairly attributed the greatest transfer problem to the managers while overcrediting their own efforts. If this self-

Figure 4.4   PERCEPTIONS OF MOST FREQUENTLY USED/MOST POWERFUL ROLE/TIME COMBINATIONS FOR USING TRANSFER STRATEGIES

		TIME PERIODS	
	Before	During	After
Manager	5/1	6/8	9/3
ROLE-PLAYERS Trainer	2/2	1/4	7/9
Trainee	8/7	3/5	4/6

Key: 1 = high; 9 = low frequency/potency

serving attribution occurred, trainers themselves may not always be as heavily involved before and during training as they assert. This would suggest that trainers might also need to expand their transfer management roles into before, during, and after time frames. We recommend that additional research be done in this area to get a more precise assessment of the impact of each role-time combination on supporting transfer.

A LOOK AHEAD

To the degree that any managers, trainers, and trainees recognize the probability of problems with transfer and see the need to work together to reduce, remove, or control for the existing barriers, they will increase the likelihood that transfer can and will occur. If they form the Transfer Partnership and develop coordinated sets of strategies, they will avoid the "If it ain't broke, don't fix it" syndrome that sometimes plagues organizations today—waiting for a major problem to occur and only then allocating costly time and effort to solve it.

Before we describe in detail the numerous transfer strategies that can be used before, during, and after training, a few important comments are in order. First, we will not be directly discussing classic learning principles related to the *design* of the learning experience itself—those instructional prescriptions that make direct contributions to the speed or efficiency with which trainees acquire new knowledge and skills. (Examples of these include the use of multiple senses, logical sequencing of material, repetition, and practice opportunities.) In our discussion of key performance improvement decisions in Chapter 3 we emphasized that appropriate design principles are essential in paving the way for transfer, and we assume that they will be followed.

Second, we will be weaving a variety of transfer strategies into each cell of the nine-cell matrix. We will show what can be done by each of the three Transfer Partners—trainee, trainer, and manager—in each of the key time periods—before, during, and after training. This cooperation, particularly between the managers and the trainer (with the appropriate involvement by the trainee), typifies the shared decisions by managers and trainers that we described in Chapter 3. That cooperation is essential for full transfer of training to occur. (However, trainers operating in situations in which decisions are not shared can still use better management of the transfer process as leverage to move toward the more effective shared relationship.)

Third, astute readers will occasionally note some natural overlap of the transfer strategies across time periods. In other words, a given strategy could be used at two different times, or even on a continuous basis across all three time periods. Similarly, a particular strategy could also be interpreted as belonging equally well in another role-related category (e.g., the trainer may initiate a transfer strategy, but the trainee implements it). Certainly a specific strategy may be effective when used by more than one member of the Transfer Partnership in more than one time frame. Further research may eventually clarify some of the current ambiguities.

Fourth, the descriptions of most strategies will be brief and straightforward because of their inherent simplicity. In other cases we have found it desirable to provide additional details or even an occasional illustration for the reader's benefit. We intend to be succinct, informative, and understandable.

The strategies included in the following chapters are not dramatic in their individual significance. We don't claim to be offering creative new breakthroughs. Instead, we view them as a wide-ranging array of simple but often overlooked techniques that have already helped many organizations to gain a greater payoff from their training dollars. We believe that there are four keys to successful use of these strategies: (1) develop the Transfer Partnership, with managers, trainees, and trainers working together to support transfer; (2) become familiar with the full set of strategies for each cell of the matrix; (3) identify those strategies with greatest potential use in the organization; and (4) systematically implement the selected strategies and monitor the results.

Reference

Laker, Dennis R. "Dual Dimensionality of Training Transfer." *Human Resource Development Quarterly* (Fall 1990): 209–223.

Part II
IDENTIFYING TRANSFER STRATEGIES

Chapter 5

TRANSFER STRATEGIES BEFORE TRAINING

To ensure that a training intervention for managers produces the payoff that is intended, strategies to transfer the learning must be carefully integrated into the instructional game plan.

— Michael J. Kruger and Gregory D. May, "Transfer of Learning in Management Training" (1986, p. 3)

KEY THEMES FOR THIS CHAPTER:

- The importance of proactively planning for transfer
- Managerial and organizational pretraining strategies that set the transfer climate
- The trainer's repertoire of transfer strategies prior to training
- The trainee's role in transfer preparation before training begins

In this chapter we will focus on a set of foundational strategies the members of the Transfer Partnership—managers, trainers, and trainees—can use to support eventual transfer. These strategies can be explored and implemented even before training begins. (Figure 5.1 shows the focus of this discussion on pretraining actions.) We will argue for the importance of taking a proactive stance toward transfer of training. Then we will systematically identify and discuss the action strategies that are most clearly in control of each role player.

This chapter focuses on the transfer strategies that precede the entry of trainees into the training experience (whether it is called a course, program, or session). These practices are listed chronologically, as opposed to those to be implemented during and following training. Pretraining strategies have another important characteristic: they accent the importance of being *proactive* regarding the entire transfer process. Members of the Transfer Partnership must anticipate and constructively confront potential barriers to transfer. In particular, being proactive is both a frame of mind and an action orientation;

Figure 5.1 FOCUSING ON PRETRAINING TRANSFER STRATEGIES

		TIME PERIODS	
		BEFORE	During	After

ROLE-PLAYERS		BEFORE	During	After
	Manager	░░░░		
	Trainer	░░░░		
	Trainee	░░░░		

it represents a guiding philosophical orientation toward always thinking ahead, as well as a set of practices designed to prevent problems.

Throughout this and the following two chapters, we have coded each strategy according to the appropriate role and timing for its use. Thus, M/B.1 is the *first* strategy presented for the *manager* to consider using *before* training. TR/B refers to strategies by the *trainer before* training, and TE/B to strategies by the *trainee before* training. Similarly, in Chapter 6, strategies *during* training by the manager, trainer, and trainee are M/D, TR/D, and TE/D respectively. Finally, strategies *following* training by the manager, trainer, and trainee are shown in Chapter 7 as M/F, TR/F, and TE/F respectively.

PRETRAINING TRANSFER STRATEGIES FOR THE MANAGER

The manager should take each strategy discussed in this section with attendant cooperation and support from the trainer. (Remember, in this book we define *manager* to include team leaders, supervisors, managers at all organizational levels, executives, and any others who represent organizational authority.) Managers need to provide and demonstrate their full support in advance of the training experience. As we saw in Chapter 4, support from the manager greatly strengthens the likelihood that trainees will apply the new learning effectively on the job. In some cases the full Transfer Partnership should be involved, with the manager initiating the action.

(M/B.1) Build Transfer of Training into Supervisory Performance Standards

Employees in organizations tend to respond best to two broad factors—what they believe is important and what they are rewarded for doing. In psychological terms, we refer to these processes as *cueing* an individual's behavior through providing some antecedent that will stimulate it, and *consequating* the individual's behavior by administering a positive response. The first action strategy to be discussed uniquely addresses both issues, though focusing primarily on the first.

We recommend that each organization review the performance standards for all of its managers and supervisors and revise those standards where appropriate. The modified performance standards should include a specific expectation that all supervisory personnel will actively support human resource development for their subordinates and be held accountable for the results. All supervisors would then realize that they would be appraised against an additional criterion—the actions they have taken to ensure appropriate training for their employees and to support the transfer of training by their employees to their job.

This strategy builds on the notion expressed in the classic story about the owner of a stubborn mule that would not pull the plow, even in response to the farmer's repeated coaxing, urging, and enticements. Becoming impatient, the frustrated farmer finally picks up a board and smacks the mule alongside its head, whereupon it obediently responds to his commands. "Why did you do that?" inquires an astonished bystander. "First," the farmer responds, "you have to get its attention!" Similarly, the organization has to get the attention of all supervisors (via the performance planning and appraisal processes) and convince them that transfer of training is important. Only then can they be expected to expend energy toward its accomplishment.

(M/B.2) Collect Baseline Performance Data

How will the organization know when transfer has occurred? It can learn this only from a comparison of pretraining and posttraining behaviors and performance data. This analysis is essential for managers and trainers to identify transfer problems and then to measure the impact of their transfer actions. This can also contribute to good research (including design, data acquisition, and data analysis) through which the HRD field can become more professionalized. A rich place to begin this process is in documenting the degree of training transfer that occurs (assuming, of course, that appropriate control groups are also assessed).

To do this, trainers and supervisors of the trainees must work together to devise measures of employee behavior/performance (e.g., job requirements) before training and gather data regarding current performance on those measures. This provides a pretraining baseline of performance information that helps to identify specific needs for training. It also generates the requisite "before" data for comparison with "after" results. Collecting baseline data may serve another useful purpose (overlapping with some of the earlier transfer strategies presented): it cues trainees on what to expect in the training program, how their performance will be assessed upon their return to work, and the likely performance goals they will have to meet following training.

(M/B.3) Involve Supervisors and Trainees in Needs Analysis Procedures

Training should be designed to solve a present or future problem, overcome a gap or deficiency, or prepare employees for future specific or general job responsibilities. Managers, trainers, and trainees (as appropriate) should participate in identifying training needs. For example, trainers might become independently aware from their examination of the organization's strategic plan that new skills will be needed when a technological conversion takes place. All aspects of this prospective need should be discussed with managers and supervisors. Trainees should be involved as well because an uninformed trainee group may be less than receptive to the accompanying training. (This is particularly important with a culturally diverse workforce; cultural differences may cause, or contribute to, the need for training.) In short, independent needs analysis by either managers or trainers would overlook important inputs that could be provided by employees and would ignore the strong desire by many employees to participate in such decisions.

To capitalize on the societal trend toward more participative management practices, trainers and managers should cooperate to use needs analysis procedures that ensure that training programs will meet high-priority needs, *as perceived by relevant decision makers and the training's recipients.* Surveys, interviews, and training advisory committees all help to meet this objective. The lesson here is straightforward: trainees will be more receptive to training (and more likely to apply it) when they perceive it meets their needs. Supervisors will be more supportive of training applications by their employees if they have had an advance opportunity to focus the training on high-priority needs they perceive. Finally, trainers will gain more credibility if the training they manage is perceived as a high-priority need by all partners.

(M/B.4) Provide Orientations for Supervisors

Another key strategy for managers and supervisors is to insist upon, and participate in, advance orientation sessions regarding the training programs to which they will send their employees. It is imperative that supervisors discover the highlights of the training so that they can cue their employees in terms of what to expect, provide a proper role model for them in terms of desirable behavior, and properly reinforce the desired behaviors following training.

These orientations, though usually abbreviated versions of the training programs, also provide trainers with a chance to pretest their material and approaches and to receive constructive feedback from line personnel.

Orientation sessions also serve as helpful refreshers for supervisors who may have forgotten key elements in the training program. They are especially useful when training programs have evolved over time, incorporating substantial revisions or replacements of content of which supervisors may be unaware. Finally, supervisors' attendance at orientations is a powerful way to show employees that the supervisors care enough about the training to spend time and effort familiarizing themselves with it. Knowing this, employees will be more receptive to the program.

(M/B.5) Involve Trainees in Program Planning

A cliché suggests that the person in the boat with you seldom bores a hole in the bottom of it. Similarly, if trainees are brought on board (directly or indirectly) to participate in the design of the training program, they will not only be less likely to sabotage it but will be more committed to learn and apply the material. The key question then becomes, "How do I get my trainees to jump aboard my program?"

One of the best ways is to *invite* them aboard. One or more trainees should be involved in the program planning (course design) process. Just as supervisors can be drawn into advisory committees to steer the direction of employee development efforts, first-line employees can participate in that process. Employees can be surveyed to determine their present work problems and concerns, diverse cultural attitudes and expectations, needs for additional skills, and task deficiencies. Later, when they see that their input was used in the course design, they will be much more committed to its goals and objectives.

Managers should also consider forming a cultural advisory board of representatives from various workforce cultures in order to provide ongoing advice and consultation on a range of cultural diversity issues, including training. The representatives should be selected by the cultural groups in the workforce, not by managers, to ensure credibility with the represented employees. Where the workforce is unionized, cosponsorship of the advisory board by the union may strengthen the board's effectiveness.

(M/B.6) Brief Trainees on the Importance of the Training and on Course Objectives, Content, Process, and Application to the Job

Employees typically respond to messages that cue them as to organizational expectations. If they sense that the training they are about to receive is perfunctory, they cannot be expected to devote much serious thought or effort to it. By contrast, they should be told in advance by an important person (e.g., their supervisor or a higher-level manager or executive) that the training session is relevant, useful, likely to improve their job skills or advancement potential, and expected to produce a measurable organizational payoff. As a consequence, trainees will be much more likely to be attentive, receptive, and willing to apply what they learn.

This strategy builds on the concept of the self-fulfilling prophecy: the supervisor increases the probability (but cannot guarantee) that trainees will use what they learn by creating an expectation in trainees' minds that the training will be a positive experience for them. Then trainees expect to find something of value in the training, watch more closely for it, and are alerted to the need to search for application opportunities upon their return to the workplace. This strategy is similar to the proven benefit of sharing training objectives with trainees: if you tell them what you expect the program to accomplish, they are more likely to marshal their energies in the same direction.

(M/B.7) Review Instructional Content and Materials

Managers and supervisors should examine the training design in detail before the program is finalized. This provides an opportunity to confirm and validate that content is based on the needs analysis to which supervisors contributed earlier. Also, their review can examine whether the course materials, structure, style, and approach are congruent with the organization's culture and with the diverse cultural values trainees may have identified.

(M/B.8) Provide Supervisory Coaching Skills

Some supervisors have never received much on-the-job coaching themselves. As a result, they may not appreciate how important their coaching is for their own employees. And because they may lack familiarity with how effective coaching is conducted, supervisors may not know the proper steps to use to coach their employees.

We recommend that organizations assess the coaching attitudes and skills of their first-line supervisors in particular. Supervisors must be convinced that even the best off-the-job training for their employees generally requires that the supervisors engage in follow-up observation, emotional support and encouragement, discussions to review the highlights of what was learned and how to adapt it to their specific jobs, and frequent praise for progress made. When there are cultural differences between supervisors and employees, supervisors must learn how to provide coaching in ways that are culturally acceptable to trainees. (Trainees may become coaches to their supervisors, to help them develop appropriate coaching methods.) Supervisors represent a potentially powerful influence for most workers, and only through individual coaching contacts can they ensure that transfer will occur. The best time to prepare supervisors for this coaching role is *before* the employees undergo their own training, so that the supportive environment will be in place upon their return.

(M/B.9) Provide Time to Complete Precourse Assignments

Increasingly, trainers are developing and using materials that provide opportunities for trainees to react to various self-assessment instruments, incidents, readings, and questionnaires in advance of training. Especially if these are lengthy, trainees may be reluctant to spend time and effort to complete them in advance of training. This is a problem for trainers who must then face some trainees who have not done the necessary advance work. No matter whether they accommodate the prepared or the unprepared group during the training course, they are in danger of losing the interest of the individuals not accommodated.

The solution, of course, lies in guaranteeing that all trainees have done the advance work required of them. Our preferred approach is for supervisors to monitor the distribution of materials, invite the trainees to complete them by a certain (pretraining) date, provide job release time for their completion, and then discuss them with the trainees prior to the training. When this occurs, the implicit message for trainees is that their supervisor deems the training to be vitally important, is well aware of what is going to happen, and will be watching their behavior upon their return to work. The training itself is likely to be more successful from an acquisition-retention-maintenance standpoint partly because of factors of repetition, "hooking" the trainees' interest, and ensuring that all trainees are starting at the same place when the training begins.

Some major organizations (e.g., Xerox and IBM) insist that trainees do their homework before attending a particular course. If they arrive unprepared, they are subject to a "send home" policy and denied the training at that time. Communication of this policy provides a powerful incentive to complete the prework materials.

(M/B.10) Offer Rewards and Promotional Preference to Trainees Who Demonstrate New Behaviors

Why should trainees expend the time and effort to adopt new work habits? Why should they discard proven and comfortable patterns of behavior in exchange for uncertain and sometimes uncomfortable approaches? Organizations must provide some rationale—explicit or implicit—for employees to change before transfer of training can be expected to occur with great predictability.

Some people change to new behaviors because they recognize that it will be easier for them to perform their jobs. Others change because they have no choice (e.g., technology-driven changes), because they are bored with the old and find challenge and excitement in the new ways of doing things, because they are receptive to direction and control from others, or only if there is an early and visible reward for doing so. For the latter, such rewards can take the form of greater economic incentives (e.g., higher bonuses for improved sales following sales training).

Many employees today have the drive to get ahead—not just economically, but also in terms of their social status within the organization's hierarchy. The prospect of future promotions is often appealing, either to escape a currently unsatisfying job or to gain prestige among their friends. Organizations have an opportunity to tap into this potentially powerful need by offering the prospects of future job promotions if trainees learn well, apply new knowledge, and practice their new skills on the job. But the connection must be clear, both in stated corporate policy and especially through everyday practice (e.g., promotional assignments). Specifically, supervisors can suggest to employees about to be trained, "If you show me that you effectively apply to the job (across a reasonable and extended period of time) what you have learned, then I will be able to recommend you for a promotion when a higher-level job classification becomes available."

(M/B.11) Select Trainees Carefully

Successful training, and its long-term application on the job, is possible only when the right people are provided with the right training (content and process) at the right time and are supported by the right kind of organizational environment. The "right" trainees are those who have an immediate (or imminent) need for new knowledge or skills to perform their jobs. Too often, trainees are selected for training for the wrong reasons—for example, "the workload was slack," or "they needed a break from their daily responsibilities," or "they had friends in Milwaukee (where the training was to be held)," or "you can never train too much." Sometimes supervisors capitulate to "want"-oriented pressure from subordinates to allow them to attend training programs in desirable locations, or because the title of the program is catchy, or because "everybody else has received training this year and I haven't had my share." Finally, trainers are all too familiar with the employee who shows up as a last-minute replacement for someone else but who has no need or desire for the training.

The lesson here is obvious. Trainees learn best, and are more likely to apply their newly learned knowledge and skills, when they recognize a current or impending need. Trainees should know the criteria for selection and view their selection as a message of positive regard for their future capabilities and contribution potential. Only those whom the supervisors honestly believe can benefit the most from training and are likely to apply the training should be selected.

(M/B.12) Arrange Conferences with Prior Trainees

"Nothing succeeds like success." The next best thing to personal success in trying a new process or skill is to hear about past successes from a respected colleague or friend. Organizations can take advantage of this cueing phenomenon by identifying workers who were previously trained and then used their training effectively, and having them meet with prospective trainees.

Prior trainees can provide important clues in terms of what to watch for, how to get the most out of the training session and materials, and how best to adapt the training to meet the new trainees' needs. Supervisors should set up mini-briefing sessions prior to training in which previous trainees share their experiences, allay the fears and concerns of new trainees, and provide a positive role model for use of the new knowledge and skills. This powerfully communicates that the organization endorses the training, that the training is relevant and useful, and that there is someone to go to for information afterward if questions should arise. Care should be paid to the selection of appropriate prior trainees; if they are not enthusiastic about their new skills, they will not stimulate enthusiasm for the training in prospective trainees.

This strategy can be particularly helpful in a culturally diverse workforce. Managers and trainers should consider selecting employees who are effective cultural role models as the first group of trainees for a new high-priority training program. Following completion of training (assuming the pilot program was successful), managers should schedule briefings by these employees with their co-workers from the same cultural backgrounds who will be trained subsequently.

(M/B.13) Send Co-Workers to Training Together

A powerful factor in inducing change within any organizational unit is obtaining a *critical mass*—creating the skills and desire for change within a large enough subgroup that the trainees can have some impact on the unit's subsequent behavior. In short, it is difficult to move a mountain by oneself. However, the incremental gain in impact from the addition of just one more pair of hands in training is substantial.

Consequently, supervisors should consider selecting not just one but two or more trainees from the same unit to attend some training sessions. In the first place, the unit immediately gains a back-up person in case one should be ill or leave the job. More important in the short run, however, is the support provided by two persons experiencing the same training. For example, people differ in their note-taking abilities and learning styles, their capacity to absorb content, and their ability to see potential applications back on the job. Some are optimists ("This is great stuff! I can use this tomorrow."), whereas others are more reserved ("I don't yet see how I can apply this to my job").

Given these inevitable differences, organizations should consciously pair the participants in advance of the training to increase the likelihood of greater transfer and impact through the support each can provide to the other. If possible, these should be compatible individuals who are comfortable working together and supporting each other. They should be briefed in advance as to why two or more are being trained concurrently and instructed in what to look for while in training. They should also be told that they will be asked to report on the training in a joint fashion after it is over and will be expected to work together in a complementary fashion on their return to the job. Then the supervisor must follow through on those commitments.

(M/B.14) Provide a Positive Training Environment (Timing, Location, Facilities)

A popular motivational theory developed by Frederick Herzberg many years ago made a key distinction between the job's context (environment) and the job's content (the work itself). Essentially, Herzberg suggested that a bad work environment distracts an employee from gaining satisfaction from the job itself. In short, employees are not motivated to high levels of performance until they have a reasonably acceptable work environment. Only then will they turn their attention toward the value of more intrinsic rewards. Consequently, organizations should assess and control the nature of the training environment. This environment, broadly defined, minimally includes timing, location, and physical facilities.

Timing. Trainees will be primed for transfer if the timing of the training is right. This builds on the concept of the teachable moment, in which employees are more receptive to training when they perceive a need within themselves and are not pressured by distractions. Therefore, employees should be selected for training when a change in technology occurs, requiring new skills; new job responsibilities are to be assumed because of transfer, promotion, or merger; or the employee's performance has been appraised as requiring substantial and sustained improvements in the near future.

Location. In some cases on-the-job training, or training embedded in the work itself, is the most effective in producing the desired new behaviors. In other cases off-site locations are beneficial, in which trainees are protected from work-related interruptions and distractions. Managers and trainers should work together to determine the most cost-effective location for each training event.

Physical facilities. Much has been written about the value of pleasant and comfortable physical surroundings during training. Experienced trainers are convinced that such features as the right colors, temperature, and shape of chairs and tables contribute to trainee learning (though there is little substantive supporting research). A disruptive or inadequate training environment not only distracts trainees but also sharply affects their attitudes toward the value of the training itself. Managers should provide a positive learning context for their trainees to demonstrate the importance of the training and create a supportive climate for transfer.

(M/B.15) Plan to Participate in Training Sessions

Supervisory presence can be very powerful in the minds of trainees. However, it takes managerial commitment and preparation to make this occur. Managers need to reserve the time to participate in forthcoming training sessions. Planning to do so will help ensure their presence at the training program.

(M/B.16) Encourage Trainee Attendance at All Sessions

In advance of employee attendance at a training session, supervisors must make it clear to trainees that they are expected to attend all sessions to receive optimum amounts of learning. They also need to view their assignment to training as equal in importance to their work assignments, not optional. They should be told that their participation in training will not be interrupted. Finally, supervisors should indicate that they expect to hear a detailed report on what the trainee gained from all parts of the training.

(M/B.17) Develop a Supervisor/Trainee Contract

Most organizations using behavioral contracts have trainers distribute these to trainees at the end of a training session (see Chapter 6). However, these are basically one-party contracts (the trainee committing to a new set of behaviors) and occur after training is completed. A more powerful approach (but one that does not preclude the later one) is to have supervisors and trainees collaboratively develop a more general contract *in advance,* specifying each party's commitment to maximizing the results of training through the active participation of each member. Figure 5.2 shows an example of a pretraining contract between supervisor and trainee.

Figure 5.2 **SAMPLE BEHAVIORAL CONTRACT BETWEEN TRAINEE AND SUPERVISOR**

EMPLOYEE STATEMENT:

I, _____, would like to participate in the following training program: _____. If selected, I agree to:

  a. attend all sessions;
  b. complete all pre-work, reading, and other assignments;
  c. actively participate in all training modules, keeping an open mind;
  d. create specific action plans detailing my expected applications of the training content, and discuss these with my supervisor;
  e. share highlights of the training with relevant co-workers.

Signed _____

Date _____

SUPERVISOR'S STATEMENT:

I, _____, the supervisor of the employee identified above, agree to:
  a. release him/her from sufficient work assignments to allow complete preparation for, and attendance at, all training sessions.
  b. attend and participate in all advance briefing sessions for supervisors.
  c. meet with the trainee following training to determine highlights of the session and mutually explore opportunities for applications.
  d. minimize all interruptions to the training.
  e. model the desired behaviors for the trainee.
  f. provide encouragement, support, and reinforcement for the new trainee behaviors.
  g. provide specific opportunities for the trainee to practice the new behaviors and skills.

Signed _____

Date _____

In summary, trainees' managers and supervisors play a key role in many ways prior to training. They can shape employees' attitudes in a positive way, they involve the trainee in setting goals for themselves following training, they make explicit promises of rewards that can be received if training is successfully transferred, and they generally encourage trainees to view training as potentially helpful in their jobs and careers. But this may still not be enough. We will now examine some of the tactics that trainers themselves might use before the first trainee appears.

PRETRAINING TRANSFER STRATEGIES FOR THE TRAINER

Trainers have several opportunities to strengthen the transfer process before training takes place. Clearly, there is overlap between some of the following trainer-controlled strategies and some of the manager's strategies discussed earlier. In fact, in some cases the only difference is *which partner*—manager or trainer—initiates the specific transfer strategy. Nevertheless, the overlapping items bear repeating here.

(TR/B.1) Align the HRD Program with the Organization's Strategic Plan

One of the strongest recommendations to flow from the HRD literature in the last decade is the admonition for trainers to link the HRD program to the organization's strategic plan. When the trainer functions as the HRD consultant (see Chapter 3), in full partnership with management, linkage with the organization's strategic plan becomes easier. The trainer is asked to contribute HRD expertise to the plan, highlighting the human resource development implications within it and helping to implement that plan. Connecting the HRD function to the strategic plan also elevates the status of HRD within the organization.

Once the strategic plan is developed, with well-thought-out HRD implications clarified, the HRD professional has the opportunity and responsibility to make all future HRD programs fit within its framework. Programs must contribute to the achievement of key priorities, just as they must address identified trainee needs. When priorities and needs are clearly linked, trainees will be able to see the larger picture and the relationship of their new learning challenges to the organization's vision and strategies. This alone can facilitate transfer of training by strengthening the perceived connection between knowledge and skills to be learned and the probable payoff to be achieved. Once more, trainers can cue the trainees to recognize that the training to be received is important, practical, relevant, and supported by the organization.

(Chapter 10 suggests ways for the trainer to build this effective Transfer Partnership.)

(TR/B.2) Involve Managers and Trainees

It is crucial that trainers involve managers and trainees in needs assessment and course design. Involvement—when it is desired, legitimate, and substantive—can produce tremendous payoffs, both from the participative process itself and from its products. Fortunately, the trainer is often in a position to initiate the involvement of the other partners. The first four key decisions on performance improvement (discussed in Chapter 3) require this involvement.

Many opportunities exist to solicit trainee input. Trainees can be interviewed, observed, surveyed, or tested to determine whether there is a need for the topic, which employees need training, or how the training methods/materials should be adapted to the trainees' cultural values. Statements of performance objectives can be assessed by a group of prospective trainees to see if they clearly communicate their intent. Preliminary course designs (individual modules, exercises, etc.) can be pilot-tested by trainee groups to measure effectiveness and to gain trainees' reactions and feedback. Trainers must recognize the great value of the input from trainees and then take the initiative to involve them in meaningful ways. When this happens, trainees will be increasingly likely to embrace the training and carry it back to the work environment.

Similarly, trainers can promote opportunities to involve managers and supervisors in needs assessment and course design processes. The best way for trainers to begin to act as full partners with managers—and to be accepted as such—is to present emphatically the results of research (see Chapter 4) that shows the potential impact of managers on transfer. Armed with this information, trainers become very persuasive in getting genuine participation by managers.

(TR/B.3) Systematically Design Instruction

Trainers, in their expert role as instructional designers, can ensure that the training program produces effective learning as well as probable retention and application. The most effective way to do this is to follow a classic instructional design process:

- identifying desirable performance outcomes
- stating trainee-oriented objectives for each session

- identifying necessary skill/knowledge prerequisites

- selecting instructionally and culturally appropriate mixes of training methods and media

- structuring the training program into discrete phases (modules)

- pilot-testing the program and revising where necessary

- evaluating the results

Essential ingredients include the creation of manageable-sized units of material, proper sequencing of content (e.g., from easy to difficult; from whole picture to components to whole picture), and a healthy mixture of instructional approaches for the sake of variety. Trainee interest must be obtained and retained. Trainees must not be overwhelmed; they must see the relevance of what they are learning. They should be actively involved in their own learning process at every step of the program. Information must be repeated more than once, and success opportunities must be provided (along with appropriate feedback and reinforcement). Although all of these factors focus on learning rather than transfer, they reflect the fact that transfer of training is impossible to imagine in the absence of effective prior learning. Clearly, one is a prerequisite for the other.

(TR/B.4) Provide Practice Opportunities

One factor in effective learning and transfer is so powerful that it merits special mention. Opportunities for practice of new learning provided during training give trainees the chance to put newly acquired knowledge to work. They represent relatively safe opportunities to experiment with new skills without the risk of error, personal harm, or destruction of important products or equipment. When properly structured and overseen, practice exercises, case studies, simulations, and other active learning approaches give trainers the chance to note individuals levels of achievement and difficulty. They also give trainees the chance to ask questions, try alternatives, and gain confidence.

The key to success lies not only in developing relevant levels of trainee skills through practice opportunities so that they can do the work but also in convincing trainees that they can benefit from doing so. Practice opportunities can demonstrate to trainees that new methods are easier, faster, or more satisfying. Meanwhile, the relatively controlled training environment can remove some of the pressure, freeing trainees not only to acquire adequate levels of skill but to commit to using those skills back on the job.

This recommended strategy eliminates one of the classic errors of some trainers who feel compelled to force more and more content material into training while sacrificing skill-building opportunities. Such thinking is seriously flawed. By contrast, a smaller amount of knowledge applied well can produce a greater payoff than a larger amount of knowledge that is never applied. Practice opportunities during training can have tremendous payoffs when transfer of training is measured.

(TR/B.5) Develop Trainee Readiness

Various methods of needs analysis attempt to identify those trainees who are, and who recognize that they are, in need of training. These methods implicitly draw on the concept of a teachable moment when trainees sense and accept their own needs. This suggests that trainees will be more receptive to training, will learn more, and will be more likely to use their new knowledge and skills back on the job if they can immediately see the value in the training to be received.

Sometimes trainers are lucky enough to catch trainees at a teachable moment in their work lives; in other cases trainers must create such moments. Trainers can stimulate trainee readiness for the learning to come by carefully preparing and distributing a number of devices designed to "hook" trainee interest in advance of the training session. This includes well-designed, culturally sensitive, and attractively packaged precourse materials distributed to trainees before the start of a formal training program. These may be background readings, feedback of supervisory performance evaluations, statements on the prerequisites to their next logical career move, provocative assertions from the CEO on the need for new skills to survive hard times, or a wide variety of self-assessment exercises that allow trainees to score themselves and identify areas of potential improvement. The main idea is to stimulate trainees to think about the subject, accept the possibility that they need to change, and commit themselves in advance to using what they will learn.

(TR/B.6) Design a Peer Coaching Component for the Program and Its Follow-Up Activities

Peer coaching, as an instructional method and support for transfer, is becoming widely used in educational and library settings. The method assists colleagues in coaching each other to apply newly learned behaviors through a carefully structured sequence. First, during the training program, participants from the same or nearby work sites agree to work together. They also agree to keep their mutual feedback confidential in order to allow a relatively risk-free learning environment. They share information on their work settings and how they plan to apply the new learning.

Back at their work sites following training, by prearrangement one trainee demonstrates the new behaviors in a work situation while the other observes and records data. Then they meet to discuss the data and give and receive feedback. Within a short time the observer becomes the performer who demonstrates the new behaviors, while the other trainee assumes the role of observer who records what occurs; they then analyze and discuss what took place, giving and receiving feedback.

Peer coaching requires that trainees be well trained in the peer coaching process (observation, data recording, giving and receiving feedback), as well as in the new behaviors they are learning. It is also vital that the trainees' participation be fully voluntary and that the organization's management give full support to the entire process.

PRETRAINING TRANSFER STRATEGIES FOR THE TRAINEE

It would be easy but disastrous to overlook or even diminish the significance of the key role player in the entire training process—the trainee. A similar oversight may be part of the overall problem of low productivity afflicting some organizations.

Little has been written about transfer strategies that trainees can take prior to their involvement in training. The dearth of substantive ideas in this domain may be a reflection of our collective failure to consider the prime role of trainees. Our review of the literature on transfer of training produced only three substantive strategies for trainees: providing input into program planning, actively exploring the nature of a training program, and readily participating in advance activities. Each of these will be briefly discussed. Astute readers may note that trainee activities often overlap with those of the organization and the trainer, as some opportunities provided by the former two groups now simply need to be capitalized on by the trainees.

(TE/B.1) Provide Input into Program Planning

Assume the following worst-case scenario. Neither the organization's training department nor its supervisory group has chosen to invite trainee input into needs analyses and program design processes. For example, "tradition" in some organizations dictates that only managers make decisions; this may have systematically excluded trainees. In other cases, an implicit corporate philosophy may suggest that trainees "don't (or can't) really know what is best for them, so why ask them?" The geographic dispersion or cultural diversity of trainees may inhibit efforts to involve them in data-gathering and other consultative processes. It is even possible that some trainee groups have been consulted in the past and either blew the opportunity or chose not to respond.

Regardless of the organization's past history, much can still be gained through trainee participation (both substantively, regarding program design itself, and motivationally through trainee "buy-in" to the process). Specifically, we suggest that *trainees* take the initiative, where necessary, to request training, identify skill deficiencies, clarify cultural differences, and suggest program features. Trainees may need to seek out their organization's training staff to provide these inputs, or channel them through their own supervisors. (Where the workforce is unionized, union representatives may be the most appropriate initial point of contact.) The results can be dramatic if the suggestions are valid and the audience is receptive; HRD programs will produce the desired learning more effectively, and the trainees will be committed in advance to transferring the newly gained skills.

(TE/B.2) Actively Explore Training Options

Assume another worst-case scenario. Employees receive a notice from their supervisor or the training department that they have been selected to attend a training session. They might agree to attend for a variety of good or bad reasons. For example, they could view the training as a change of pace, a chance to relax for a day, entertainment, a possible source of new ideas, or a chance to escape from a negative work environment. Alternatively, they may be unwilling to participate but realize that they have no choice but to attend.

An alternative scenario exists, however. The trainees may decide to explore the situation actively in advance by plying their supervisors, trainers, or prior participants with meaningful questions, such as those shown in Figure 5.3. In this way the trainees can take control and gain additional understanding of what is to come by asking key questions and pressing for answers.

(TE/B.3) Participate in Advance Activities

The final suggestion we have for trainees is to commit themselves to use all advance materials available to them. This might include absorbing back-

Figure 5.3 SAMPLE EXPLORATORY QUESTIONS FOR TRAINEES TO ASK

"Why was I chosen for this program?"

"What can I expect to learn relevant to my job?"

"What is the weakest part of the program?"

"What support can I expect for using the material when I return to my job?"

"What opportunities will there be for me to begin using my new skills immediately?"

"Whom can I use as a role model?"

"Are there modules that will be inappropriate for me?"

"Is there some other background that I should acquire first?"

"What kind of behaviors should I exhibit in the program so as to maximize my learning?"

ground readings, studying technical manuals, completing self-inventories, taking basic tests of knowledge, constructing case illustrations from their own experience, or analyzing generic case histories. If these methods are not being used, trainees might take the initiative to request such items from the organization. The predictable by-products will be a greater degree of trainee commitment to the program's success and consequent likelihood of using the material presented.

SUMMARY

To make transfer of training occur, the first important time to focus transfer strategies is *prior* to the training itself. This is consistent with a proactive approach—one that is designed to make things happen according to a master plan. There are opportunities for all three role players to be involved, and we fully endorse this three-way partnership. The next chapter will move the discussion onward in time to those strategies appropriate for application during training.

References

Herzberg, Frederick. *Work and the Nature of Man.* Cleveland: World, 1966.

Kruger, Michael J., and Gregory D. May. "Transfer of Learning in Management Training: Building the Payoff into the Instructional Design." *Performance and Instruction Journal.* (April 1986): 3–6.

Chapter 6

TRANSFER STRATEGIES DURING TRAINING

Q: "How does top management [at Motorola] show its support for training?"
A: "The first is by our example. We participate. We go through training our-
selves to set an example."
  — William Weisz, Chief Operating Officer, Motorola

KEY THEMES FOR THIS CHAPTER:

- The importance of supplementing effective learning processes with con-current transfer programs

- Taking managers of trainees from behind the scenes and placing them in visible transfer management roles during training

- Providing trainees with tools to help them plan their own transfer process.

In this chapter we move to the second major time period in which transfer actions can be implemented—the time during which trainees are being trained (see Figure 6.1). Of the three time periods, this may be the briefest; many small-group activities last only a few hours, and some on-the-job train-ing and many workshops and seminars last just a few days (although some other on-the-job courses, like apprenticeships, may last for years). The short duration of much training provides both a great opportunity for *focus* of ac-tions to support transfer to the job and a sharp limitation on the *number* of actions that can be taken. Again, we will systematically discuss the action strategies that are most clearly in control of each role player: manager, trainer, and trainee.

Figure 6.1 FOCUSING ON TRANSFER STRATEGIES DURING TRAINING

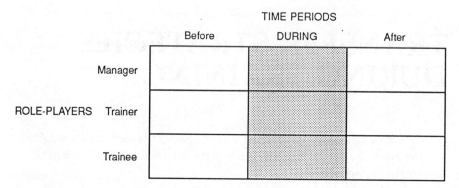

TRANSFER STRATEGIES FOR THE MANAGER DURING TRAINING

(M/D.1) Prevent Interruptions

Very little is more distracting to the trainer in charge, the trainee involved, and other trainees than to have one or more trainees interrupted during a training session. Sometimes these interruptions are initiated by the trainee, as when an individual slips out of a session periodically to make a phone call to the office. Many times the interruption comes from co-workers who stop by to ask a work-related question. Secretaries deliver messages to trainees, who sometimes feel compelled to make immediate responses regardless of whether or not a true crisis exists. On other occasions an interruption is pre-planned, as when two trainees are assigned to a training session but only under the condition that one or both return for staff meetings or other necessary tasks.

These and other types of work-related interruptions have many direct and indirect effects. The trainer may become frustrated and even lose the sense of continuity, rhythm, and "flow" that was being established in the program. The other trainees, distracted from the learning experience by multiple disruptions, may wonder how important their own continuous attendance really is. The trainee involved, of course, is likely to miss key facts and principles, involvement in important group exercises, useful illustrations, or relevant materials. Although the trainee may try to catch up after returning, the learning experience is inevitably diminished.

All of these distractions detrimentally affect application of learning to the job in two ways. First, the content will not be learned by the trainee(s) as well as it should be. Second, allowing such interruptions to occur sends an implicit message that the program is not really important. Consequently, trainees may be less motivated to apply what they have learned back on the job.

The solutions are straightforward. First, management must establish and follow a policy that *no interruptions will be allowed during training sessions.* Secretaries, co-workers, the trainees, and the trainees' supervisors must be informed in advance that only in true emergencies will messages be allowed to be delivered during a session; all messages must be held until break times.

Second, training sessions that involve significant organizational, group, or individual change (e.g., strategic planning, team-building, attitude shifts) should be held away from the work site whenever possible. This eliminates the casual drop-in conversations from co-workers and the spontaneous return by trainees to their work areas during breaks. It also makes the supervisors of trainees realize that they can't easily summon the trainee back to the work site when "something important comes up." Although all three Transfer Partners are involved in making this policy work, primary responsibility lies with the *managers* of the trainees, who must actively intervene to reduce or eliminate such interruptions.

(M/D-2). Transfer Work Assignments to Others

Many trainees dread attendance at training programs—not because they don't appreciate a break from work activities, exposure to new ideas, and a chance to improve their skills, but because they are concerned about the inevitable mountain of work that will confront them upon their return from the training program. This can have a depressing effect at just the moment you want them to enthusiastically apply their new learning. It also creates a potent and very real barrier to their immediate application of new ideas and skills. Under pressure of a work backlog, trainees are likely to revert to previous well-practiced skills and not try new ones.

The solution is largely under the control of trainees' direct supervisors. The supervisor must take responsibility for arranging for a capable substitute to handle the bulk of ongoing chores while an employee is participating in a training program. Ideally, such work coverage should continue for a brief period following the trainee's return to work (though this can be costly). A respite from a heavy workload would make it easier for the trainee to begin applying improved methods (which usually take more time, until new habits are solidly established). A supervisory practice of providing workload relief for a trainee will usually be accepted by co-workers temporarily sharing the burden as long as they recognize that sooner or later they will receive a similar benefit.

(M/D-3) Communicate Supervisory/Managerial Support for the Program

One of the most effective tools for convincing trainees that what they are learning is important and endorsed by the organization is to see and hear management support the program. ("Management" means not only supervisors but also top managers such as CEOs.) Trainees observe, listen, and sense what is important when those above them speak and act. This is the process of *social learning,* in which trainees acquire key inputs through observing others.

What are the signals that supervisors and managers can send to trainees to convey the message that what they are hearing and doing is important?

- Attendance at training sessions

- Active participation in open discussions to show endorsement of desired practices

- Acceptance of training roles in which the supervisor/manager presents some of the material

- Public/private pronouncements of support for use of new knowledge and skills

- Visible and consistent demonstration of the desired new behaviors.

In effect, the supervisors and managers must model what they want their trainees to accept, doing so through direct verbal and behavioral endorsement of the new learning. Taking the time to participate actively in the training sends a powerful message of support to trainees.

(M/D.4) Monitor Attendance and Attention to Training

HRD professionals work hard to design training that involves trainees interactively and accommodates various learning styles. However, trainees are affected by many other factors external to the training situation: family or health problems, grievances with the organization or co-workers, and so on. As a result, trainees sometimes exhibit dysfunctional behaviors—inattentiveness, conversational disruptions, napping, or session-skipping—in spite of the best efforts of trainers to keep them constructively involved. When these attendance-related and attention-related behaviors occur, they detract from the potential learning of all trainees and the subsequent transfer to the workplace. Trainers may not have the authority, flexibility, or time to intervene in such situations.

A supervisor or manager who participates in all sessions of the training can help to forestall or handle dysfunctional behaviors by taking disruptive trainees aside to explore their problems. Time demands may prevent a supervisor from attending all the training sessions in which various employees are involved. Nevertheless, if trainee attendance is considered truly important, some action is required to assure trainee presence and attentiveness.

A low-cost alternative to total involvement is for the supervisor to systematically drop in for brief periods. When this responsibility is shared by several supervisors all of whom have employees participating, the individual burden is rather light. This drop-in process alerts trainees to the fact that their supervisors support the training and value the potential learning. If a behavioral problem occurs, one or more supervisors can intervene before it gets out of control. Although this may appear to be a negative action (trying to "catch trainees doing something wrong"), drop-in visits by supervisors primarily provide the opportunity to reinforce desirable behaviors on the part of trainees.

(M/D.5) Recognize Trainee Participation

As the training program draws to a close, another useful tactic for supervisors (or higher-level managers) is to participate in the creation and distribution of certificates of attendance to trainees. This formally signifies their satisfactory completion of the training and simultaneously responds to the fact that most employees are hungry for some form of recognition. Furthermore, that desired recognition is often most powerful when it comes from valued sources.

It takes little effort to collaborate with the trainer in the design of a suitable certificate. (Inexpensive word-processing programs can easily create certificates, such as the example shown in Figure 6.2.) Perhaps the organization's print shop can tailor-make a more professional-looking set for each program if that is desired. Attractive frames make it more likely that trainees will hang the certificates in their work areas for all to see. Supervisors and managers should be asked to be present for a few minutes at the end of each program to distribute certificates or other forms of recognition to each trainee. This does not require much time, effort, or cost but it provides trainees with a "trophy" to show to co-workers and family and a daily reminder that the organization supports application of what they learned.

(M/D.6) Participate in Transfer Action Planning

Without exception, every training program should include some type of action-planning session for trainees to plan how to transfer their learning to the job. In Chapter 8 we will describe a special type of action-planning

Figure 6.2 SAMPLE CERTIFICATE

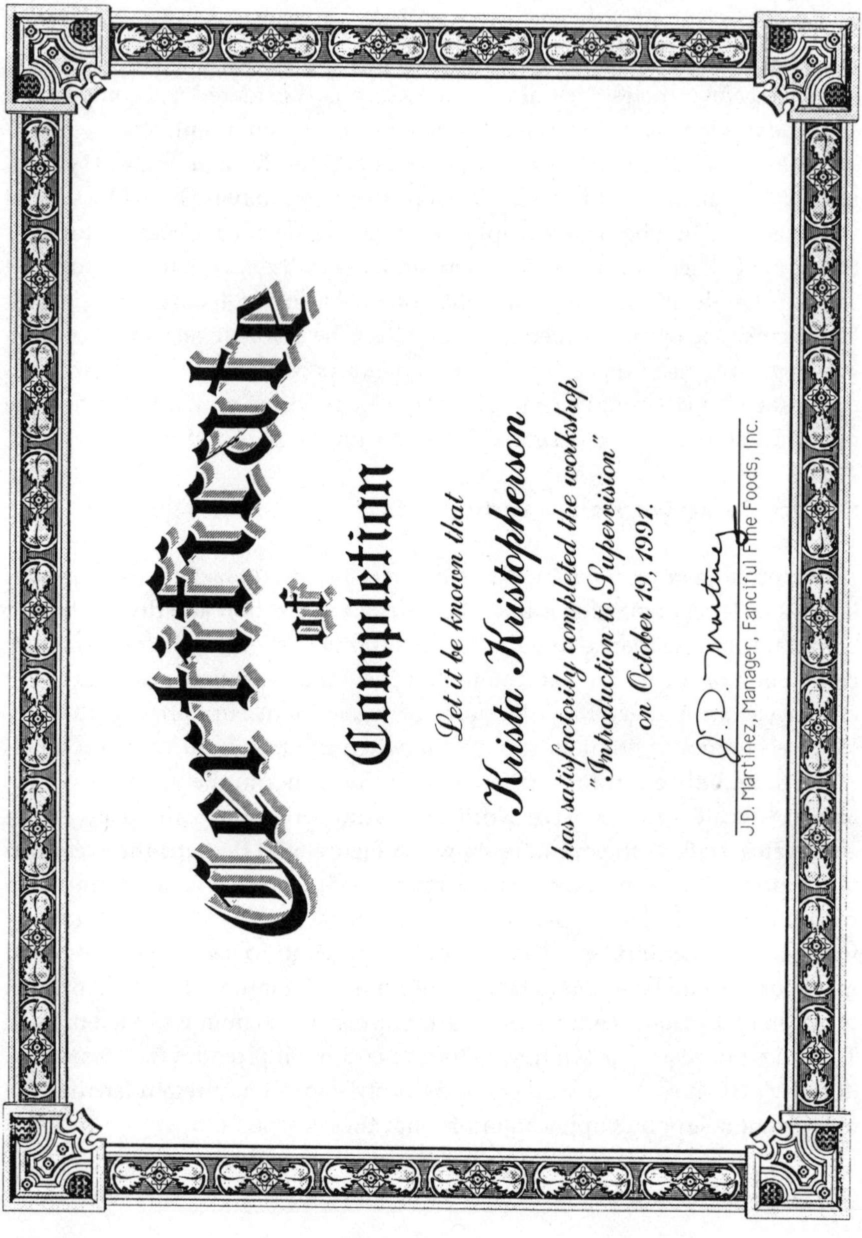

Certificate
of
Completion

Let it be known that

Krista Kristopherson

has satisfactorily completed the workshop
"Introduction to Supervision"
on October 19, 1991.

J.D. Martinez

J.D. Martinez, Manager, Fanciful Fine Foods, Inc.

session, a "relapse-prevention" module, for use at the end of a training program. For relapse prevention or any other type of action-planning session, the supervisor's presence and active participation is vitally important. Here is a brief overview of how the session might work.

On a structured group or individual basis, supervisors meet with the trainees at the end of the program but before the trainees have returned to the work-site. The supervisor and trainee review the learning objectives, and the trainee describes what was learned to reach each objective. Both discuss how the learning can be applied to the current job. The supervisor endorses, elaborates on, or suggests modifications to the employee's action plan and then identifies the resources and support that will be provided to help the employee succeed in applying the new behaviors.

The action plan, including commitments to behavioral change by the trainee, and support to be provided by the supervisor, should be written in the form of a contract and signed by the parties. (This is a natural extension of the contract discussed in the previous chapter and illustrated in Figure 5.2.) Together, the two parties resolve to collaborate in making the training pay off through improved or modified work habits/behaviors. They also openly talk about the potential problems each sees and how they will prevent, minimize, or overcome such problems. Finally, they would be wise to discuss and establish a timetable and system for periodic review of trainee progress toward achieving improved behaviors.

(M/D.7) Review Information on Employees in Training

While employees are away from the job and being trained, supervisors should review background information on each trainee (e.g., previous work assignments, prior training, cultural background and values, behavioral deficiencies, significant strengths). This will help supervisors to make better decisions about impending job assignments and hence increase the match between what is currently being learned and the opportunity to apply it.

This is particularly important for new hires, who will arrive at the work site for the first time following training. The more that supervisors can learn about their employees' backgrounds, cultures, skills, and experiences, the better they can plan to support entry to the new job. As the workforce becomes more ethnically, racially, and socially diverse, this preliminary planning becomes critically important. Supervisors may need special training and action planning themselves to recognize and constructively address cultural differences that may arise in language, work habits, and expectations of others. The first impression that the new employee has on arriving on the job will set the tone for the working relationship between employee and supervisor. A well-informed supervisor will support the new employee's entry to the job in culturally acceptable ways.

(M/D.8) Plan Assessment of Transfer of New Skills to the Job

Before trainees arrive back on the job, supervisors should also consider how they will assess the trainee's degree of transfer of new skills. An evaluation process should be designed which provides the supervisor and the employee with objective feedback about use of training-related knowledge and skills. Even knowing that their behavior will be monitored may independently encourage greater transfer by trainees (a cueing mechanism relying on the power of expectations and the self-fulfilling prophecy, as discussed in Chapter 5). Regular evaluation and feedback on employee use of new skills will encourage trainees to continue working on transfer of new skills.

TRANSFER STRATEGIES FOR THE TRAINER DURING TRAINING

There are two primary ways in which the trainer, as manager of transfer, can support transfer during the training program. (1) If the trainers deliver the training, they can make sure that appropriate transfer strategies, from among those to be discussed later, are implemented. (2) If the training is delivered by others (managers, supervisors, subject-matter experts, external consultants, other employees), the trainer can plan in advance with those involved in delivery and monitor the actual training to be sure that transfer strategies are implemented.

In either case, the trainer must be the advocate for transfer, to ensure that the demands of assuring effective training *delivery* and immediate *learning* do not overwhelm and distract those delivering the training from the necessary concentration on eventual transfer to the job.

A trainer can use several strategies during training. The astute reader will note that there may be substantial overlap among strategies by the trainer and the trainee (and, occasionally, the manager). The primary difference lies in who takes the initiative for an action. Following are a set of trainer-oriented transfer strategies for use during training.

(TR/D.1) Develop Application-Oriented Objectives

Most instructional designers and trainers prepare and use lesson plans on a formal or informal basis. These plans denote both *process* objectives (what the *trainer* will do during the training session) and *product/outcome* objectives (e.g., what the trainees will know and be able to do immediately when the session is over). These are important tools for guiding trainers in their choices and actions and for letting trainees know what is to be achieved in a particular module.

We suggest that a third type of objective be developed and communicated to trainees: *application-oriented objectives.* These are behavioral statements of what the trainees should do once they return to their jobs (assuming that opportunities will be provided there). Application objectives are invariably more skill directed or performance oriented than other types, which may focus more on knowledge, facts, procedures, and nonbehavioral objectives such as understanding, awareness, or even appreciation. In essence, application-oriented objectives place specific pressure on trainees to take what they have learned and put it to use. They are the product of knowledge, skill, opportunity, resources, time, and willingness to use the training.

By preparing and sharing application-oriented objectives with trainees, the trainer is cueing the trainees to think beyond the current session. On-the-job use of the new material is emphasized, and trainees can even be encouraged to tailor the objectives to fit their own situations. In addition, the trainer would be wise to explain how initial attempts to apply the new skills might be only partially successful, and thus how the shape of the extended "learning curve" might be a bumpy one at first, requiring perseverance. The entire lesson for the trainees, then, is to get them to look ahead and begin thinking about future applications.

(TR/D.2) Manage the Unlearning Process

Recently one of the authors was asked by an elderly uncle to step into a Ford pickup truck and pull a camping trailer about 50 miles to a new site. Here is his report of the incident:

> "I agreed to do so, although I hadn't driven a standard-transmission vehicle for over thirty years. I got into the truck, shifted into first gear and accelerated, then jerkily moved it into second gear and sped up some more, and finally jammed the shift lever down into third gear (high). I cruised somewhat nervously down the highway, a bit uncomfortable with having a trailer closely following the truck and being unable to see behind me. Soon, however, I lapsed into my usual long-distance-driving state of quasi-consciousness and let my mind wander across many unrelated thoughts.
>
> After awhile, I caught up with a school bus that was making its afternoon rounds of dropping off children at their country homes. After a few miles, the bus driver slowed, turned on flashing signals, and projected the "Stop" arm. Having maintained a safe distance, I felt no immediate alarm, although my mind instantly recognized that the additional inertia of the trailer would

increase my normal stopping distance. I moved my left foot from the floor to the brake and pressed lightly on it. No reaction. "The brakes must need a little adjustment," I thought, and I pressed the pedal half-way down. Still no reaction occurred, and I was closing the distance between me and the school bus. Now almost fully alert, I pressed the pedal anxiously to the floor. "I have no brakes!" I almost screamed to myself.

Suddenly (and fortunately) my brain took complete charge and rescued me and others from complete disaster. At almost the last possible moment my brain instructed my *right* foot to lift from its position hovering above the accelerator and move to the actual brake pedal (not the clutch pedal which my left foot had by now pushed nearly through the floor). Heavy pressure on the true brake pedal stopped the truck safely a few feet behind the halted school bus. I was angry with myself and yet relieved, and shook so badly that I had a hard time bringing the truck and trailer up to speed to complete my journey. But I *had* learned a lesson that day about unlearning—one which trainers should heed.

As a "trainee" on automatic transmission vehicles for many years, I had learned a bad habit—using my left foot to brake the vehicle. Then when I found myself in a standard-transmission truck, I failed to recognize the need to *unlearn* my previous habit of left-foot braking. Although I unconsciously knew how to start and stop the new truck I was in, my previous habits interfered with the application of current knowledge.

Trainers need to recognize that trainees seldom come to them with a clean slate; rather, they are a product of years of experience and habits. Sometimes these acquired practices interfere with new learning and its application to the job. As a minimum, trainers need to empathize with trainees in the difficult task of confronting the old habits and work with them to let go of those old habits before new methods of behaving can be effectively acquired and used. For some learning objectives, exercises may need to be included in the training design to help trainees consciously unlearn old behaviors in order to develop new ones.

(TR/D.3) Answer the "WIIFM" Question

Joel Weldon, an outstanding motivational speaker and trainer, suggests that every member of his audience (and all of your trainees) is constantly tuned in to radio station WIIFM. This station sends them a signal, constantly asking the question "What's in it for me?" Bluntly speaking, many trainees want to know what they will gain for the investment of time and energy in changing their behavior. Trainers should anticipate and answer this question.

After sufficient consultation with trainees' line supervisors or managers, trainers should share with trainees what they can expect to gain from a behavioral change. Will the new work method be less taxing on them? Will it be safer? Will it provide more variety or greater freedom for the performer? Will the increased quality or speed of work result in personal financial gain? What is the reason they should discard the old and adopt the new? Trainees have a high degree of self-interest at heart, and this should not be dismissed as being unreasonable. Until trainers develop and share acceptable responses to the WIIFM question, they will find themselves facing trainees who are at best neutral and at worst highly resistant.

(TR/D.4) Provide Realistic Work-Related Tasks

Much of the earliest writing about transfer of training by E. L. Thorndike and others (see Irwin Goldstein, 1974) focused on two ways to help trainees apply what they had learned. The first was *transfer through principles,* in which trainees were given broad guidelines or generalizations (e.g, "most mechanical problems are caused by the lack of preventive maintenance") and expected to retain them and determine how the guidelines could be used later in more concrete applications. If trainees learned these principles, presumably they could not only identify their applicability on the job but use them effectively in specific circumstances. However, it is often very difficult for some trainees to see how broad principles apply to a wide range of new and specific job challenges.

Second, transfer was to be facilitated through the use of *identical elements.* Using this approach the training design approximates or incorporates as many facets of the trainee's work tasks as possible, thereby making transfer almost a nonissue. The secret to the identical elements approach is to design and use realistic work tasks during training, or at least simulations into which a high degree of reality is built. Extreme examples are pilot training simulators with realistic aircraft-related stimuli provided by sight, sound, and physical movement. More common illustrations include any "vestibule"-type training (off of the immediate job site, but working on actual machines and tasks) such as financial institutions often use for their teller trainees before placing them in front of customers. In short, instead of just talking about the tasks, explaining them, or using case examples and subsequent discussions to elicit what trainees think they would do, trainers should have trainees performing typical work tasks in a controlled and protected environment. This proves quite effective, particularly when careful job analyses preceding the training design allow training to cover a high proportion of actual job responsibilities so the trainees can later see the identical elements between training and job.

(TR/D.5) Provide Visualization Experiences

Many people are familiar with the power of positive thinking. Similarly, Denis Waitley, a well-known author and motivational speaker, suggests that "people move in the direction of their dominant thoughts." Both of these popular concepts suggest that our minds control our bodies, as illustrated by athletes who envision themselves performing flawlessly and standing in the winner's circle at the completion of their competition. Building on this idea in the following way can help trainees more effectively transfer their newly acquired skills to the job site.

Through many of the actions presented in this book, trainers can suggest that trainees prepare a small number of *behavioral transfer intentions*—resolutions or commitments to apply some key concepts or skills that they learned during training. Trainees are then asked to visualize or imagine how they would look, sound, and feel if they were doing the job task using these concepts and skills, and what the effects would be in terms of job performance. Focusing exclusively on a few key concepts or skills (dominant thoughts) and envisioning what the experience and the results would be like (visualization), the trainer is encouraging a mild form of self-hypnosis among the trainees. Trainees in turn are committing themselves to a small number of significant behavioral changes and visualizing themselves performing the task as they are trained to do *before they return to the job site*. Then, when they actually return to the job, they will effectively have a *déjà vu* experience (the feeling that they have been there before) as they practice the new skills. This process of seeing themselves as effective performers will help them be effective.

(TR/D.6) Give Individualized Feedback

Most people are hungry for feedback. (Former New York City Mayor Ed Koch became famous for asking wherever he went, "How'm I doing?") People need feedback to learn how others view their behavior, and they use feedback to learn, grow, and adapt to a changing environment or new set of expectations. Feedback that is timely, specific, individualized, constructive, focused, and requested by the recipient can prove extremely helpful in stimulating and supporting individual growth.

Not all trainers have the luxury of being able to provide one-on-one feedback. The trainer may be present for only a short time, the training program may be too brief, or there may be such a large number of trainees that individual attention is impossible. Occasionally, however, a trainer may have the opportunity to provide even a brief feedback-related statement to one or more trainees.

When this opportunity occurs, the trainer can shift more toward *feedforward guidance* (that which explains what to do) than traditional feedback (on what was done). In using feedforward guidance the trainer reflects on how the trainee is doing but points all comments toward what the trainee should do and how he or she might perform back on the job. The comments should be tailored to the individual so that trainees can make a direct connection between the constructive comments and their own behavior. The comments should also be future-oriented so that trainees can focus on the right way to perform on the job.

(TR/D.7) Provide Job Performance Aids

"I knew how to do it once, but not anymore." "I remember hearing it, but it slipped my mind." "I have a vague recollection of how it was supposed to be done, but I can't pin it down." "I forgot!" These comments sometimes are heard from our trainees mere days after returning from training sessions. They attended, they were attentive, they absorbed the content, and they probably even passed the end-of-course examination. Yet, shortly thereafter they offer lame statements explaining why they aren't using what they learned.

Some memory loss is inevitable. Employees' brains are bombarded with innumerable stimuli on a daily basis. Each new input received tends to crowd out from the conscious mind what was deemed important only moments before. Is it true that trainees must "use it or lose it?" Perhaps not, if trainers take more responsibility for facilitating transfer of training.

A key element in helping trainees retain what they learned and use what they know is to provide memory cues and "crutches." *Job performance aids* are invaluable tools not only to slow memory loss but also to cue trainees to keep applying new learning. Job aids are typically a printed or visual summary of key points or steps essential in the performance of a job. They may be kept at the trainee's desk or work site as a daily reminder, posted on the wall, or carried in a pocket. Examples include highlights of relevant sections of a labor contract for first-line supervisors, key steps in an effective sales presentation for sales representatives, or reminders of proper telephone etiquette for customer service representatives. An enlarged illustration of a pocket-sized job aid—the procedures for performing cardiopulmonary resuscitation (CPR)—is provided in Figure 6.3.

(TR/D.8) Actions under Control of Trainers or Trainees

The remaining approaches that trainers can implement during training to stimulate transfer are similar to those to be discussed in greater detail on

Figure 6.3 CARDIOPULMONARY RESUSCITATION (CPR) JOB AID

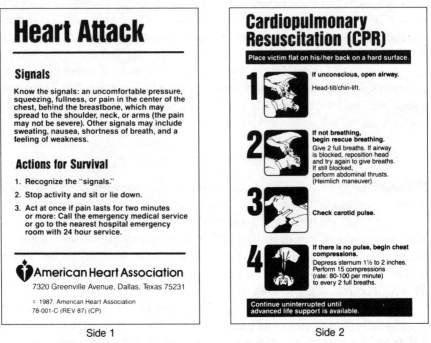

Heart Attack

Signals

Know the signals: an uncomfortable pressure, squeezing, fullness, or pain in the center of the chest, behind the breastbone, which may spread to the shoulder, neck, or arms (the pain may not be severe). Other signals may include sweating, nausea, shortness of breath, and a feeling of weakness.

Actions for Survival

1. Recognize the "signals."

2. Stop activity and sit or lie down.

3. Act at once if pain lasts for two minutes or more: Call the emergency medical service or go to the nearest hospital emergency room with 24 hour service.

American Heart Association

7320 Greenville Avenue, Dallas, Texas 75231

c 1987. American Heart Association
78-001-C (REV 87) (CP)

Cardiopulmonary Resuscitation (CPR)

Place victim flat on his/her back on a hard surface.

1 If unconscious, open airway.
Head-tilt/chin-lift.

2 If not breathing, begin rescue breathing.
Give 2 full breaths. If airway is blocked, reposition head and try again to give breaths. If still blocked, perform abdominal thrusts. (Heimlich maneuver)

3 Check carotid pulse.

4 If there is no pulse, begin chest compressions.
Depress sternum 1½ to 2 inches. Perform 15 compressions (rate: 80-100 per minute) to every 2 full breaths.

Continue uninterrupted until advanced life support is available.

Side 1   Side 2

Reproduced with permission. © "Heart Attack Signals and Actions for Survival wallet card," 1987. Copyright American Heart Association.

strategies by trainees. The only difference involves who initiates the process. Trainers can

- (TR/D.8) Provide notebooks, preprinted sheets, and opportunities for trainees to systematically note new ideas and their potential applications in an "Ideas and Applications Notebook" during training

- (TR/D.9) Create opportunities for trainees to establish support groups both for learning together and for encouraging transfer once they are back on their jobs

- (TR/D.10) Help trainees prepare group action plans in which trainees exchange ideas on what skills they see as most applicable to their jobs and how they collectively intend to use them

- (TR/D.11) Have each trainee create an individual plan of specific actions to be taken to transfer new skills to the job; obtain a copy from each and mail it back to the trainee in a few weeks

- (TR/D12) Design and conduct a relapse prevention session at the end of the training program (preferably with the trainees' supervisors participating) to help trainees anticipate the potential barriers to transfer and plan how to prevent or overcome them. (Although this is a legitimate trainer-initiated transfer strategy during training, we believe it is important and unique enough to merit a separate chapter; see Chapter 8.)

- (TR/D13) Help trainees negotiate a "contract" with their respective supervisors specifying what they propose to do differently upon their return to their jobs and requesting specific forms of support from their supervisors

TRANSFER STRATEGIES FOR TRAINEES DURING TRAINING

In an organization with a Type C relationship between manager and trainer (see Figure 3.1), the manager, supervisor, and trainer work as partners to make all major training decisions. This includes the fifth decision—planning and implementing the transfer management process (see Figure 3.2). In organizations with effective transfer management, the trainee is brought in as the third Transfer Partner to participate in strategies that may be initiated by the other two partners and to undertake other strategies individually. These individual strategies by trainees are the focus of this section.

However, in organizations still following Type A or Type B relationships between manager and trainer, transfer is typically overlooked as an issue. In these situations the trainee may not get much support for transfer of training from either manager/supervisor or trainer. Under these conditions the trainees may have to assume increased responsibility not only for their own learning but also for constructing a motivational process to ensure that transfer takes place.

In Type C relationships, in which managers and trainers share responsibility for important training decisions, trainees still have an important role in supporting their own transfer of learning to their jobs. This section outlines seven key strategies that trainees might initiate on their own, or in collaboration with other trainees, as part of their Transfer Partnership role.

TE/D.1) Link with a "Buddy"

One relatively easy strategy is for each trainee to identify one or more other trainees with whom a supportive linkage can be established. This often occurs naturally during the training, either as a product of seat selection, task assignments (in which trainees are paired off to work on joint projects), or concurrent attendance by two employees from the same work unit.

The "buddy" process is straightforward and powerful. It is based on the psychological process of making a *commitment* to another person. In short, Jerri is more likely to engage in a new behavior if she has previously (and publicly) promised Merrilee that she will do so. In return (according to the social *norm of reciprocity*), Merrilee will feel an obligation not only to support Jerri in her efforts to apply what she has learned but also to make her own commitment to change.

However, buddy linkages require that someone take the initiative. In this example, either Jerri or Merrilee must step forward and either ask the other for help and support or offer hers first. We believe that buddy linkages are strongest when there is an ongoing work (or social) relationship, when contact and communication are relatively frequent and easy, and when some concern for the other's welfare (success in transferring new skills) is reasonably strong.

An extension of the "buddy" concept is the formation of the entire group of trainees into a *learning community*, whereby all participants share responsibility for one anothers' learning and performance. Testing and application of new learning becomes a group goal, with all trainees participating and taking responsibility for their own (and others') learning

(TE/D.2) Maintain an Ideas and Applications Notebook

"I heard a lot of great ideas, but I'm not sure that I can remember them all," commented Maria. "The concepts were interesting, but I don't see how I can use them in my job," added Craig. Kent then piped in with his own reaction, "I wish they had provided more hand-outs listing the important principles and how to use them."

The reactions by Maria, Craig, and Kent are not unusual, at least among inexperienced workshop participants. A trainee who may not have been in school for several years may have experienced some loss of memory sharpness, or trainees may have gotten out of the practice of converting general principles into specific practices, or they may not have the self-discipline it takes to develop comprehensive notes from training presentations, even if hand-outs are provided. What can they do now?

We suggest that all trainees request a notebook and sheets of preprinted forms adapted from the example provided in Figure 6.4. They might call it an "Ideas and Applications Notebook" and encourage each other to use it throughout the workshop. Trainees can develop an early example of what an

Figure 6.4 IDEAS AND APPLICATIONS NOTEBOOK

Date _____   Program_____

| CONCEPT/PRINCIPLE (What I heard/learned) | MY APPLICATION OF IT (How I intend to use it on my job) |

1. _____   1. _____

2. _____   2. _____

3. _____   3. _____

4. _____   4. _____

5. _____   5. _____

6. _____   6. _____

7. _____   7. _____

8. _____   8. _____

9. _____   9. _____

10. _____   10. _____

idea and its application might look like and then share it. During the workshop, trainees can take time to share and discuss their recent entries.

Trainees can use the notebook to sharpen their own attentiveness to what is being said and to take responsibility for identifying applications to the job.

When they have accepted this responsibility, they will listen carefully to relevant ideas and then use their skills and experience to convert those ideas into applications to the job. The notebook provides a self-discipline mechanism encouraging trainees to look for useful ideas throughout the training program, instead of waiting until the program is completed and then relying on their recall capabilities. Finally, the notebook sheets also give a visible record that trainees can show to their supervisors as a basis for transfer-oriented discussions on their return to work.

(TE/D.3) Participate Actively

A Chinese proverb suggests, "I hear and I forget; I see and I remember; I do and I understand." This proverb captures the spirit of active learning through direct involvement. Trainees should capitalize on the opportunity to become involved in oral discussions and skill practice sessions. Even though they may risk appearing ridiculous or failing to perform to the level their own expectations, they will find that the benefits usually outweigh the costs by a wide margin.

Trainees should assume some responsibility for making the session meet their own needs through the questions they ask. When opportunities for active participation emerge, they need to respond by testing new thoughts, challenging ideas, questioning the presenters, offering tentative conclusions about applications, or exploring for weaknesses. The learning that takes place through active engagement of their minds will be far more memorable, as well as better tailored to their own needs. As a consequence, trainees will be better prepared to apply what they have learned.

TE/D.4) Form Support Groups

Programs such as Alcoholics Anonymous have long recognized the tremendous merits of support groups for initiating and sustaining long-term behavioral change. *Support groups* are collections of two or more individuals who all have somewhat similar needs and who agree to meet periodically to discuss current problems and ways of solving them. In the meetings members can receive encouragement for experimenting with new applications of the ideas, principles, and skills they acquired. Trainees can form support groups to meet during the training period and, if possible, to continue meeting after return to their jobs.

Unfortunately, many leaderless or structureless groups lose their energy for meeting fairly soon. Trainee support groups must confront the same problem. It is usually helpful to establish a standard pattern of meeting times (weekly or monthly) as well as to identify an agenda, structure, and possibly a discussion leader. In addition, support group members can agree that they are not limited to contacting each other only during meetings but may call one another in the interim to check on progress, offer reinforcement for a success, or ask a question. Support groups can be very effective in helping a trainee to see the value other participants find in a program and providing psychological support for trainees' early attempts to experiment with new behaviors.

Even the best-organized support groups falter after a period of weeks or months. This should not necessarily be seen as failure. It may be that the support group met a short-term need for some trainees in testing and practicing new behaviors, and the support is no longer needed once the new behavior comes more easily. It is also possible that some trainees drop out of the support group because the new learning is too difficult to maintain. In either case, the support group has probably met some important needs and need not carry the burden of solving all problems.

(TE/D.5) Plan for Applications

Goal setting is one of the most potent motivational tools. Trainees can build goal setting into any training workshop by commiting themselves to sit down for a few moments at the end of the training session to answer the question, "What will I do with what I have learned?" In responding to this question, the best goals are typically written, specific, brief, action oriented, target dated, short term, and concrete. For example, Renee may decide that by the end of next month she will apply two of the newly acquired statistical techniques to analyze and reduce her scrap rates at least 15%.

Application planning is best done immediately following training (if it hasn't already been done throughout the workshop via an Ideas and Applications Notebook). Again, the goals will be more forceful for guiding the actions of most people if they are then shared with a significant person. Finally, they should be posted in a prominent place (on one's desk or at one's workplace) and referred to frequently.

Application planning builds on the concept of *self-management*—the idea that most adults are capable of, and enjoy, managing their own work performance. The steps involved are simple and clear:

- Setting specific goals and measurable objectives

- Identifying desired personal rewards

- Establishing contingent connections between achieving goals and objectives and receiving rewards

- Engaging in the planned actions

- Obtaining feedback

- Receiving the valued rewards

Many trainees would prefer to manage their own behavior in this way (self-management) rather than being under the control of someone else.

(TE/D.6) Anticipate Relapse

Few trainees are perfect. Despite the best of intentions, most will find that once they return to their jobs, they occasionally revert back into previous patterns of behavior. These slips are to be expected and are not inherently dangerous to the maintenance of a new behavior. However, they can become so if the employee *interprets* them to mean that behavior change will be difficult or impossible. In that line of thinking, a slip may be interpreted as a character failure, and the employee finds it easier to allow the single lapse to slide into a total relapse. (In Chapter 8 we present a special type of action-planning session for trainees, called "relapse prevention." This is the best strategy we know of to help trainees maintain new behaviors in work environments that do not strongly support the new learning. However, if the training design does not include such a module, trainees can still use some of the techniques on their own.)

Since slips are natural and predictable for fallible humans, the most effective preventive strategy is to *anticipate relapses*. In this procedure the trainee engages in an internal dialogue (self-talk) that goes like this: "I fully intend to set aside my old habits and practice the new skills, but, it's likely that I will occasionally slip into the previous practice. When I do so, I will not judge this to be a serious negative event. I will simply laugh at myself and then rededicate my efforts to beginning a new and stronger attempt at behavioral change. I will not allow a single lapse or two to give myself permission to relapse back to previous (and less effective) behaviors."

Relapse anticipation can also be supplemented by the trainees' brainstorming of the kinds of problems they expect to encounter as they try to transfer the training. Trainees must anticipate that there will be barriers to transfer, identify specific barriers, and develop action plans to confront and overcome each one. Both relapse anticipation and relapse action planning are more constructive ways to confront the reality of expected slips than the naive assumption that the road to successful application on the job will be smooth and trouble free.

(TE/D.7) Create Behavioral Contracts

Many seminars and workshops close by allowing time for trainees to reflect on what they have learned and how to use it. Some trainers even provide a blank form called "A Letter to My Boss." The form (see Figure 6.5) encourages trainees to identify the most significant behavioral changes they will make as a result of the training and share these with their supervisor in writing. It also invites a reaction and possible modifications from their boss, and then issues a specific request for support. After these behavioral contracts are written, trainees insert them into envelopes and address them to their supervisors. Then they are collected and mailed. (*That* creates commitment!)

The most important elements in this process are that the trainee's supervisor becomes aware of what the employee learned (and perceives as valuable), recognizes that the employee desires to change, and is asked to "buy into" the changes and provide concrete support for them. In short, this form may serve as the first step in an ongoing dialogue in the future, as supervisor and employee continue to share information and feedback on the employee's progress toward the desired changes. Although the form is simple, the idea is a potent symbolic element that helps get both parties committed to a significant change. Note that although the form is often developed and distributed by trainers, the trainee plays such a key role in its completion and subsequent use that we have included it in the trainee-controlled set of transfer strategies.

SUMMARY

In many ways the time period during which trainees are actively involved in the training represents a potent opportunity for stimulating transfer of training. If the training is delivered away from the job site, trainees have been temporarily released from their job duties and pressures. They may also have made some degree of commitment to learning new ideas and skills, and they are under the motivational influence of the trainer and/or others who deliver the training. If the right trainees have been selected and the training is sensitive to trainee cultures and just in time to meet their needs, there is a valuable "window of opportunity" to accent the idea of transfer. It is not only a teachable moment but a potentially viable opportunity for alerting trainees to the need to use what they are learning. A collaborative (Type C) effort among

Figure 6.5 A LETTER TO MY BOSS

Dear _____ :

I have just recently completed a workshop/course/program called _____

_____. Overall, I found it to be a worthwhile experience.

More specifically, I have resolved to make the time and expense pay off for my organization by committing myself to introduce the following new practices (or changing my behavior in these ways):

1.

2.

3.

4.

I would like to schedule a brief conversation with you when I return from the program, to explain these further and seek your reaction. Then, assuming that we agree these are desirable, appropriate, and high-priority changes, I will be asking for your direct support in helping me successfully transfer these ideas to my job in the following ways:

1.

2.

3.

4.

(Signed)_____   Date _____

manager, trainee, and trainer in focusing on transfer can help produce the results needed.

References

Galagan, Patricia. "Focus on Results at Motorola." *Training and Development Journal* (May 1986): 43–47.

Goldstein, Irwin I. *Training: Program Development and Evaluation.* Monterey, Calif.: Brooks/Cole, 1974.

Waitley, Denis. *Being the Best.* Nashville, Tenn.: Oliver Nelson Publishing, 1987.

Chapter 7

TRANSFER STRATEGIES FOLLOWING TRAINING

If executives mouth support for training, but act as though training is not important to them, no one will misinterpret the message.
— Patricia S. McLagan, "Top Management Support"

KEY THEMES FOR THIS CHAPTER:

- Prime role of managers in posttraining transfer programs
- Trainee self-management in the absence of other forces favoring transfer
- Trainer involvement after the training is completed

Research by William Byham, Diane Adams, and Ann Kiggins on transfer of training in supervisory skills (e.g., handling emotional situations, overcoming resistance to change, and improving employee performance) suggests that three factors support transfer: if trainees have *acquired* new skills, if they have the *confidence* to try the new skills on the job; and if the new skills are *positively reinforced* (1976). This conclusion points out the multiple roles involved in successful transfer (the *trainer* supporting skill acquisition, the *trainee* having the self-assurance to attempt application of the skills, and the *manager* providing feedback and reinforcement). It also accents the need to follow up even the best of training with a systematic program of activities to ensure retention and application. This chapter deals with those follow-up activities which can produce at least incremental, if not significant, payoffs after the training session is over (see Figure 7.1).

Again, we want to emphasize that the trainer and manager (and, in some situations, trainees) should carefully select transfer strategies based on the culture of the organization, the nature of the training, and the characteristics and cultures of the trainees (see Newstrom and Lengnick-Hall, 1991). No single set of strategies is equally appropriate for all training situations.

Figure 7.1 FOCUSING ON TRANSFER STRATEGIES FOLLOWING TRAINING

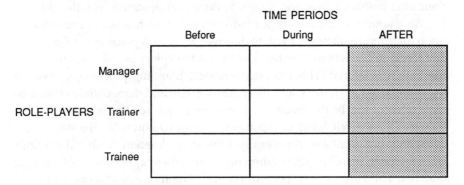

POSTTRAINING TRANSFER STRATEGIES FOR THE MANAGER

Our research on transfer of training (see Chapter 4) revealed two key facts. First, the involvement of the trainee's supervisor following training is one of the three most potent role-time combinations for any type of intervention. Second, our data showed that the involvement of supervisors following training was perceived to be the least frequently used of all nine possible combinations of role players and times.

When we combine these two conclusions, a sad picture emerges: transfer-related strategies with significant payoffs are not being used as often (or as well) as they could and should be. More positively stated, there is a tremendous potential in many organizations for transfer improvement by focusing (especially) on strategies by managers after training.

(M/F.1) Plan Trainees' Reentry

Years ago, at the beginning of the United States' space program, jokes were told about other countries that were ahead of the United States in their ability to place astronauts into orbit around the earth. The punchline, however, was that the other countries had not yet figured out a way for safe return of the astronaut through the earth's atmosphere without burning up the space capsule and sacrificing the life of the astronaut! Similarly, reentry planning for trainees is essential.

In the previous chapter we advocated that supervisors make plans (while employees are being trained) to smooth trainees' transition back to jobs and facilitate use of their new skills. This process of reentry planning should continue after training is over and should be done participatively with the trainees.

An example is the supervisor who sits down with trainees immediately upon their return, debriefs them to discover what took place, identifies mutually foreseen barriers to transfer, and begins to explore possibilities for use of the training material. This interactive reentry planning process conveys the importance of the training and its on-the-job use and demonstrates that ultimate transfer will be the result of a partnership between the manager and the trainee. One explicit focus of this meeting is to acknowledge the differences between the training environment and the work situation, so that the trainee will recognize the difficulties inherent in immediate applications of training material. The purpose is to prevent rapid deflation of expectations and energies that might otherwise come about as a result of trainees encountering the less-than-ideal receptivity of the workplace (and, sometimes, colleagues).

(M/F.2) Psychologically Support Transfer

After the trainee returns to the job from the training program, the supervisor should conduct another series of one-on-one meetings with the trained individual. The express purpose of these meetings (a supplement to the reentry meeting) is to *communicate support* for transfer through messages such as "I'm aware you are trying to apply your training," "I'd like to hear from you what you find to be working and operationally useful to us," "I want to endorse your using what you have learned," and "Tell me what I can do to help you apply what you learned." In short, the supervisor needs to immediately assure the trainee of continuing mutual interests in transfer and of the necessary support being provided. Also, the supervisor and trainee should refer to and monitor the previously developed concrete action plan for using new knowledge and skills. (The action plan should have specified what was to be done, by whom, when, and how.) Finally, the supervisor should set up additional follow-up meetings at periodic intervals for further information sharing, problem solving, and support of the transfer effort. (Note that involving the trainer in this planning by supervisor and trainee can provide important additional support. See "Posttraining Transfer Strategies for The Trainer" later in this chapter.)

(M/F.3) Provide a "Reality Check"

An effective transfer strategy by managers and supervisors is providing a *reality check*. Managers should remind trainees on their return to the job that it will seldom be as easy to apply new skills as trainers made it sound, that there will inevitably be difficulties, frustrations, and setbacks, and that the path to success will be rocky and circuitous. Trainees sometimes need to be brought back down to earth, and have their expectations for what they can accomplish become more realistic.

Supervisors can do this through individual, supportive conversations with trainees. The objective is to maintain the trainees' enthusiasm for applying new ideas and skills while also sensitizing them to the fact that their progression will not be linear. In fact, trainees will probably have a mixture of mini-successes and mini-failures in the first weeks and months following training. The simple message to convey is that the supervisor *wants* them to change to new and preferred ways of thinking and behaving, but they should not expect the process to be easy.

Trainees will need to be psychologically prepared for a characteristically challenging journey. The supervisor needs to manage employee expectations carefully to prevent the disappointment and withdrawal that sometimes accompanies short-term failure. (This strategy echoes the concepts of "relapse prevention," to be described in detail in Chapter 8.)

(M/F.4) Provide Opportunities to Practice New Skills

During the first posttraining meeting, the supervisor must ensure that all of the key ingredients for successful transfer are provided. Trainees must have the *opportunity* to apply new knowledge and skills, and they must *perceive* that they have that opportunity. Supervisors must assign trainees to the kinds of jobs, tasks, or special projects that will not only give them the chance to use what they learned but actually require them to apply it.

Besides providing the opportunity for practice, these assignments also help to prevent the natural tendency for trainees to attribute the reason for not transferring knowledge and skill to the actions of their supervisor (e.g., "She never gave me the chance to use it," or "I wanted to try it, but the training didn't fit my job responsibilities.") Managers give trainees some control of their transfer destiny by assigning them to viable tasks that allow them to experiment with new learning. A college athlete who is taught to slam-dunk the basketball but then relegated to the soccer team cannot directly transfer the dunking skill even though both capability and desire might be present. Opportunities must be provided to trainees, and be perceived and accepted by them, to allow transfer to occur.

(M/F.5) Have Trainees Participate in Transfer-Related Decisions

A body of research literature strongly supports the benefits of allowing employees to participate in certain decision-making processes. Not only can better quality decisions often be obtained, but the employees are more likely to accept the decisions and commit themselves to successful implementation. (See, for example, the ideas of Victor Vroom and Arthur Jago, 1988, and Edward Lawler, 1986.) In fact, organizational use of participative methods is becoming so widespread that a societal norm is virtually in place, suggesting that employees have the *right* to expect participation at work—to be empowered.

Supervisors can capitalize on the benefits of participation to encourage transfer of training by involving newly trained employees in deciding where and how transfer can best take place. Supervisors can ask trainees, "What opportunities exist in your job for applying what you have learned? Which of the new skills do you think have the greatest potential payoff? Do you see any cultural barriers to transfer of new skills, and how should we deal with them? What actions do you intend to take this week that utilize your training? What improvements and results do you expect to produce, and how will I know they exist?" The key lies in getting trainees to commit to behavioral change from within themselves, rather than simply being asked or urged to do so from without. The participative process, if properly used, can do this.

(M/F.6) Reduce Job Pressures Initially

Elementary physics suggests that any object (or trainee) at rest tends to remain at rest unless sufficient force is applied to put it into motion. Sometimes, however, we forget that there are different ways to start an object (or trainee) moving and keep it moving. For example, consider the case of two individuals who have a contest to see who can move a railroad car by hand a hundred feet down the tracks. One takes a position behind one car, huffs and puffs, straining mightily, and slowly edges the car toward the finish line. The other individual surveys the task carefully, moves to the front of the other car, carefully oils all the wheels and the tracks, and then pushes the car toward the finish line. Guess who finished first?

This example provides a lesson for managers of returning trainees while reminding us of a fundamental concept from Chapter 2. There are many ways to induce change, and it occurs not merely from pushing harder. Sometimes it is more effective to reduce the restraining forces. Managers need to make it easier (initially) for trainees to attempt transfer, and they can do this by temporarily reducing the job pressures that newly trained employees bear. This gives the employees a period to experiment, to "get up to speed," and to take time to solidify new patterns of behavior. When this is supplemented with extra attention and positive support from their supervisor, it is more likely to result in effective transfer.

(M/F.7) Debrief the Trainer

Trainers often accumulate rich data (comments overheard, anecdotes, observations, and inferences) as they watch, teach, and interact with trainees. It may be fruitful for supervisors to arrange a debriefing meeting with trainers to seek out such information. Supervisors might ask, "What went well? What skills were clearly learned? What didn't go so well? What skills do trainees still need help to master? How did the trainees respond to the workshop? Who showed resistance, or had serious reservations? How can I help those who did?" Answers to questions like these, plus all other trainer observations, will indicate ways in which future training sessions might be revised, and also guide the development of a follow-up plan for each trainee.

(M/F.8) Give Positive Reinforcement

Reinforcement is the systematic application of a positive consequence to a trainee, contingent on the demonstration of a desired behavior. It requires some knowledge of what the trainee would perceive as positive. (This can be complex if there are cultural differences among groups of trainees on what is appropriate reinforcement.) Usually a few words of praise given by a respected individual (such as the supervisor) are sufficient. Effective reinforcement also requires administering the reinforcement systematically (e.g., only following observation of the desired behavior) and making clear the connection between the behavior and the reward. Under these conditions positive reinforcement can be highly effective for cementing a pattern of desirable work behaviors and stimulating their repetition.

Earlier in this book we presented as the most significant barrier to transfer of training the lack of positive reinforcement for new job behaviors. Supervisors who choose to use positive reinforcement will find it a powerful device for encouraging employees to continue applying their new knowledge despite early frustrations and temporary setbacks. Most employees require some emotional support as they venture into new arenas, and a consciously designed and carefully administered program of positive reinforcement can pay off. Often all that is necessary is a word or two of praise for early success.

(M/F.9) Provide Role Models

Consciously or unconsciously, employees often pattern their behavior after that of those around them. This is called *vicarious learning*—using observation of others to acquire new experiences and skills. Supervisors can capitalize on vicarious learning by providing positive role models for employees.

In many work situations the most powerful role model for the trainee is the supervisor. The earliest research that we have found on transfer of training (by Fleishman, Harris, and Burtt, 1955) showed consistent desired performance on the job only by trainees whose supervisors demonstrated those behaviors. Explicit coaching and reinforcement by the supervisor greatly enhances the effectiveness of role modeling.

As another source of role models, returning trainees can be assigned to another, more experienced employee. This senior employee helps to explain how and why to behave while demonstrating effective performance to the trainee. (If possible, the senior employee should be from the same cultural background as the trainee, or fully sensitive to it.) The role model or coach gives direct, on-the-job guidance and immediate correction if necessary. The trainee can see first-hand how the job is performed and receive ongoing encouragement as well. By formally assigning a role model to the new trainee, the supervisor takes control of a process that might otherwise occur only by chance.

(M/F.10) Schedule Trainee Briefings for Co-Workers

Another strategy for inducing positive transfer of training also has a side benefit for other employees. Some off-site training is prohibitively expensive, and not all employees can be sent. Shortly after an employee returns from such a training workshop, the trainee can be asked to present a briefing to co-workers on the training's objectives, content, methods, and outcomes. (Ideally the trainees would have been told in advance of this expectation, so they won't be caught unaware of the responsibility upon their return.)

This strategy has several advantages. First, people often learn the most when they teach others. In this transfer strategy the trainees know that, on return to work, they will change roles from trainee to trainer of colleagues. Consequently, it is more likely that the trainee will listen, organize thoughts, and look for ways in which the training can be used by the trainee and others in his or her organization. This deepened concentration increases the trainee's likelihood of retention. Also, the focus on identifying ways in which others might find the training useful heightens the trainee's sense of commitment to transfer.

There are other important advantages. If a single employee who has undergone training can then train others in the key concepts of a costly program, the effective (per capita) costs of training will greatly diminish. In addition, the effective benefits of the training can be magnified through the combined efforts of multiple employees using the new knowledge or skills. If this is handled well, it will also contribute to building a "community of learners" who work as a team to develop one another's skills in a cooperative manner.

(M/F.11) Set Mutual Expectations for Improvement

Challenging goals can be powerful motivational tools if they are accepted by the employees involved. If those goals were not established before training took place, they should be set on the trainee's return to the workplace after training. At this point the supervisor can explain the importance of the new skills in improving productivity, the total (direct and indirect) expenses involved in training, the need to show a positive return on the investment in the relatively short run, and the ways in which the training can be applied to the individual's job. Together the supervisor and trainee should then set measurable goals or objectives for the new levels of job performance that are expected following application of the training. For best results, these should be jointly agreed on and committed to by both parties in writing, with a schedule laid out for periodic follow-up sessions.

(M/F.12) Arrange Practice (Refresher) Sessions

Occasionally employees are trained to do things that they are only infrequently called upon to perform. This is especially true for crisis-related skills that both the organization and the individual hope will never be needed. Examples include being able to apply cardiopulmonary resuscitation (CPR) for an individual who has collapsed, landing an airplane under adverse mechanical or weather conditions, and containing an oil spill when a tanker runs aground. For noncrisis but infrequent situations, other skills will almost certainly be needed, such as calming an irate customer or briefing top-level management on short notice. In this case training can be given if the need arises. Unfortunately, "once trained, always capable" is not generally true.

For those skills that are highly important but seldom used, the issue of *skill perishability* becomes critically important. This concerns the length of time it takes a skill to decline below competency level after it has been initially learned. For perishable/critical skills, trainees need some reminders of the key steps involved. Although some life-saving and safety procedures require periodic practice (e.g., fire drills) and formal recertification (CPR), many other tasks don't. For these, supervisors should arrange periodic review and practice sessions. These should be as carefully designed as the original training, with performance objectives and tailored methods and materials. They are often much briefer than the original training because in-depth explanations and demonstrations are not needed and question-and-answer sessions are typically shorter. The practice session may be self-instructional. The main focus is to give trainees an opportunity to refresh their memories about the key points involved, proper procedures, and sequence of steps. These may be relatively low-cost sessions, but they are crucial for ensuring transfer when the appropriate problem presents itself.

(M/F.13) Provide and Support the Use of Job Aids

Sometimes the solution to a problem lies in front of us and yet we fail to see it. Frequently job aids (e.g., checklists, flow charts, diagrams) are provided by trainers to assist in trainee transfer, but they suffer from nonuse. They may stay in desk drawers or in the folders or three-ring binders the trainees brought home from the workshops, or they may have been discarded. Worse, they may be posted in prominent places in front of employees and still not be recognized. (Common examples are the "Safety Glasses Required" signs that fail to remind employees to protect their eyes until it is too late.)

If job aids are available, the supervisor's job is to make sure they are used. The supervisor can *ask probing questions* ("What was the third step in that procedure you learned last week?"), *model the process* ("I still carry my reminder card around in my shirt pocket every day so I can refer to it."), or directly *request the behavior* ("Please post the list of major parts in front of your workstation so you won't forget to include any of them"). Some organizations have created spontaneous games in which employees are rewarded (e.g., with a pair of movie tickets) if they are carrying the appropriate job aids with them when confronted by any member of the management team.

If job aids have not been provided in the training session, the supervisor can develop them. In many cases proficient employees have developed their own job aids (sometimes called "cheat sheets"). A contest can be held for the best job aid ideas or examples; these can be combined and made available to all employees.

(M/F.14) Support Trainee Reunions

Some very positive things can happen during training programs. Excitement is generated; new ideas are shared; improvements are foreseen; bonding occurs among trainees; "buddy" relationships and support groups are sometimes created; and trainees reflect on their work practices. The energy thus created is not easily sustained, however, when trainees return to their workplace faced with daily operational pressures. What can supervisors do to help trainees retain some of the positive energy?

Supervisors can encourage and facilitate "reunions" of trainees. Scheduled usually on company time, these sessions allow trainees to share success stories, address and solve problems, remind one another of commitments they made to try new ideas, and mutually reinforce one another's early transfer of new skills. It may be possible for one or more of the trainers to attend and participate. This gives the trainees a chance to seek additional clarification, to bounce ideas for application or adaptation off the trainer, to receive a brief refresher on key concepts, and to provide some additional feedback to the trainer as well.

The major purpose of the reunion is to increase the trainees' commitment to apply what they know and to regain some of the earlier motivational energy they had for making transfer occur. Recreating some of the elements (e.g., renewed contact with co-trainees and trainer) that generated that energy initially can be as productive as a married couple returning to the site of their honeymoon to rejuvenate their relationship.

(M/F.15) Publicize Successes

Noted author and speaker Tom Peters suggests that organizations should "celebrate small wins." He explains that while it is imperative that herculean efforts receive big awards and grand recognition, "numerous awards for small acts of heroism are at least as important" (1987, 310). Certainly individual attempts to transfer new skills to the workplace, though expected of all trainees, are important enough to receive some level of recognition.

Supervisors should first determine what are personally and/or culturally preferred forms of recognition for their employees. Based on this analysis, supervisors can help to publicize the successful transfer of skills by commending worthy employees during departmental meetings, by providing individual praise in front of employees' peers, by inviting the corporate communications staff to write feature articles for the company newsletter on selected employees, or by nominating successful trainees for "Employee of the Month." All of these approaches rely on the old axiom that the sweetest sound to the human ear is the sound of one's own name, and this is even more powerful when combined with praise. Supervisors who publicize examples of successful transfer are doing two things: reinforcing the desirable behavior by the employee named, and indirectly inviting other employees to demonstrate their own effective use of training.

(M/F.16) Give Promotional Preference

Most employees want to improve themselves, both by gaining additional skills and by increasing their earnings capabilities. One of the more potent ways in which supervisors can encourage transfer of training is to implement a *preferential promotion policy* that specifically incorporates completion of relevant training courses and successful transfer of that learning to employees' jobs. When employees see that application of training knowledge is rewarded with career advancement, the message will be clear, and transfer should occur with increasing regularity.

POSTTRAINING TRANSFER STRATEGIES FOR THE TRAINER

It is too easy for classroom trainers to let go of trainees once they walk out the door of the workshop or classroom. Many factors contribute to this. For example, some training sessions are so brief, or training groups so large, that it is nearly impossible for trainers to get to know their trainees. This lack of personal contact diminishes the trainer's felt need to sustain a relationship and follow up on trainee use of new skills. Also, trainers often feel that they have little impact on what trainees do at the job site; in fact, they may be viewed there as an unwelcome interference into the supervisor's domain. Finally, trainers are sometimes scheduled so tightly that they virtually run from one workshop to the next, or to last-minute preparations for the next one.

The consequence of these pressures and distractions is both predictable and dysfunctional: *trainers often do not support the transfer process following the training itself.* This can also be true of coaching and other individualized or nonclassroom training. The next series of transfer strategies is designed to provide trainers with ideas and tools to help make their training pay off. If at all possible, for many training situations trainers must stay involved even after training is completed.

(TR/F.1) Apply the Pygmalion Effect

Drawn from Greek mythology and incorporated into Henry Higgins's experiment with Eliza Doolittle in the classic musical *My Fair Lady*, the Pygmalion Effect suggests that one's expectations about a future event can often affect the likelihood of its occurrence. This concept suggests that whatever is consciously or unconsciously foremost in someone's mind will influence how that person spends his or her time and energy. In psychological terms, this becomes a self-fulfilling prophecy, in which one's expectation that something will happen affects the priorities and energies one devotes to making it happen.

In the training domain, a trainer initiates this process after the training is over by telling one or both of two key parties (the trainee and the trainee's supervisor) that the trainee now has the requisite skills and capabilities to be a successful performer. In effect, the trainer is implanting a mindset within the listener that the trainee will surely transfer the training (assuming that proper on-the-job support and opportunity are provided). This is especially powerful when both the trainee and supervisor believe it.

Opportunities to convince trainees that they can and will transfer the training abound throughout training; good trainers allow and create success opportunities during training on a progressive basis. At the conclusion of training the trainer helps trainees develop action plans to transfer training and makes encouraging remarks. For a limited period after training is over, trainers might attempt to systematically call or visit the trainees to renew the message. (Obviously, this is not always feasible in large or geographically dispersed organizations.) Trainers can also arrange a visit with supervisors following the training of their employees to convince them that successful performance is likely to occur if (and only if) the supervisor allows, encourages, and actively supports it.

These positive expectations are important prerequisites to behavioral changes by trainees, and trainers should capitalize on opportunities to induce such a Pygmalion Effect. This bolsters the results of their training and helps trainers in two ways: by increasing the probability of measurable effects of the training and by building positive feelings of support for the trainers' efforts among two key constituent groups.

(TR/F.2) Provide Follow-Up Support

When two or more people, through constructive mutual interaction on a joint task, produce more or better-quality products than they would have produced through working alone and then combining their results, *synergy* has occurred. Interaction with others—those who are similarly trained (like the "buddies" discussed earlier) or who have similar goals and technical vocabulary—produces a positive motivational effect on those involved and helps to create a synergistic outcome.

Trainers can help to induce synergy among their trainees back on the job in a number of ways. They can take the initiative to contact individual trainees or small groups after they have returned to their jobs. By redefining their roles from strictly trainers/presenters to *facilitators of behavioral change on the job*, they can reach out and help a synergistic effect occur. Trainers must remember that they often have a persuasive influence over trainees, but that this influence declines quickly on the trainees' return to their workplaces. If trainers would take the time to call or visit trainees and work with them briefly as on-the-job consultants, they will support achievement of synergy through joint efforts with trainees and hence be more likely to achieve successful transfer.

Questions that trainers can ask of individual trainees back on the job include: "How are things going in your attempt to transfer some skills? Which of the major ideas I discussed in the program have you used so far? What has been the result? What keeps you from using items A, B, or C? On which topics would you like some further clarification or review? What can I do to help you transfer what you have learned successfully?"

(TR/F.3) Conduct Evaluation Surveys and Provide Feedback

Evaluation surveys help to remind trainees of what they learned and the need to apply it. Here are two ways to use them. First, after a short (e.g., 30–60 day) period following the training session, trainers can design and distribute a simple survey questionnaire to each of the participants. They can include both questions with *quantifiable* responses (e.g., "On a scale of 1 = low to 10 = high, to what degree have you been successful thus far in transferring what you learned to your job?") and questions that ask for more *qualitative* reactions (e.g., "What difficulties have you encountered so far in trying to use some of the new skills you acquired?") The survey process itself can spark trainees' interest in transfer and reenergize their commitment to continue their transfer efforts.

The trainer should then tabulate, combine, and interpret the results and send a summary of the highlights to the entire group. This can be done in a periodic newsletter or bulletin, for example. A specific trainee can be highlighted by reporting the ways in which that trainee has been successful in changing his or her behavior and achieving results. Trainers might enclose copies of course highlights or additional content material for independent trainee reading, or other news items that support the transfer of skills.

Throughout these processes, trainers can capitalize on opportunities to refresh trainees' memories, and also to cue trainees to look for ways to apply the training concepts and skills. At the same time, positive publicity given to successful trainees provides social reinforcement for their achievements. The key to successful use of surveys and feedback as transfer strategies lies in their *timing* (early, and frequent), their provision of *models* for trainees to emulate, and the public *recognition* given to those with early accomplishments to report.

(TR/F.4) Develop and Administer Recognition Systems

We suggested earlier that most trainees are hungry for recognition of their efforts and achievements. We recommended that trainers orchestrate ways to recognize trainee achievement during the training itself through friendly group competitions, praise for individual progress, and distribution of certificates of completion at the end of training. Although research suggests that truly potent recognition comes immediately after the accomplishment itself and is presented by respected individuals (e.g., one's boss), other forms of recognition can also be useful.

Trainers can suggest an annual employee recognition event to the organization's executives, in which all those who successfully completed and transferred skills from a series of related training programs are applauded. Trainers can also talk with supervisors of individual trainees to suggest ideas for creating and distributing more tailored forms of recognition for successful transfer.

A wide variety of certificates and plaques can be created and awarded with some degree of fanfare to recognize completion of training, transfer of skills, and productivity gains. This can be effectively (but carefully) done on a humorous basis, through creation of a plaque for "Spending more hours in training than working" for a good-natured employee. These can be accompanied by balloons, a celebratory cake, and a demonstration of genuine camaraderie at the workplace, all with the objective of making known to the trainee and others that training *and* transfer of skills to the job are endorsed, important, and noticed. Trainers may not be able to control such events, but they can play important roles in stimulating their occurrence.

(TR/F.5) Provide Refresher/Problem-Solving Sessions

Training sessions, for a variety of organizational reasons, are often packed into a tight time frame. Many ideas and concepts are presented, and trainees may not have adequate time to think, absorb, and reflect on what they are hearing and doing. A few weeks later their memories begin to dim, and what once seemed totally clear has become fuzzy in their minds. Unless trainees individually take the initiative to review their materials, question their supervisors, or contact their trainers, they may soon lose the essence of what was communicated to them. And without recall/retention, application is virtually impossible.

The first line of defense for trainers is, of course, to redesign the training. Nonessential content should be eliminated, practice/application sessions should be built into all sessions, and trainees should be helped to develop action plans for transferring important skills to the job.

However, total redesign may be politically or economically impossible. If the "fuzzy outcome" scenario is seen as highly probable, trainers can combat it through the preparation of simple and straightforward refresher/problem-solving courses. The purpose is to provide a brief but coherent summary of the essential concepts and skills learned earlier. In addition, however, this should be followed by a problem-solving session in which participants can share tales of their successes for other trainees to emulate, as well as discuss why they haven't yet been as successful as they wish in transferring the course concepts. The minds and energies of other trainees, as well as the trainer, can then be brought to bear on ways to prevent or circumvent such difficulties. Refresher courses thus incorporate the basic principles of repetition, modeling, and reinforcement, as well as helping the trainee to address some of the inhibiting factors that act as barriers to successful transfer.

POSTTRAINING TRANSFER STRATEGIES FOR THE TRAINEE

A powerful argument can be made that trainees are the ones in ultimate control of determining whether or not training gets transferred to the job site. In order for trainees to apply new skills to the job, some degree of the following elements must be present within trainees: the *ability* to apply a new skill, the *opportunity* to do so, the *confidence* to try, and the *perception* that there is some value (personal or organizational) from doing so. Also, they must be able to remember what they learned (retention) and find some internal or external support for their actions. Four specific strategies under the control of trainees are presented here.

(TE/F.1) Practice Self-Management

Psychologically mature employees have the capability, and can learn, to manage *and* sustain their own efforts to apply training concepts and skills. They do this by taking the responsibility for monitoring their own behavior both before and after the training program. They set goals for themselves, initiate behavior changes, watch for opportunities to apply their new learning, and collect objective data where possible to substantiate behavioral changes. These activities help employees to achieve a state of *self-management*, which is often necessary in the absence of direct support provided by many supervisors.

Self-management, however, is extremely challenging for trainees to achieve. The pressures of work, cultural insensitivity in the work environment, lack of support or even resistance by supervisors and co-workers, and difficulty of self-reinforcement are significant barriers to transfer of skills on one's own. This situation calls for use of a "relapse prevention" module during the training program, as described in Chapter 8.

Whether attempted on one's own or as part of a relapse prevention effort, self-management should be accompanied by a significant and critically important follow-up activity. Periodically these self-managing trainees need to pause and reflect on their new behavior patterns. They need to recognize and applaud their own efforts, improvements, and results. In effect they should be engaging in a "self-stroking" process, giving themselves both intrinsic and extrinsic rewards for satisfactory performance. The intrinsic rewards include internal feelings of satisfaction ("I'm OK; I've become a better employee, my self-esteem has improved because of my new performance level"). The extrinsic rewards are often even broader in scope ("I'll treat myself to something good this weekend for having applied three of the new statistical techniques for improving product quality during the past two weeks; I'll ask for that extra day off I have coming to me through 'comp' time, now that I've completed the special project for my boss"). The key is that the individual takes responsibility for providing his or her own rewards and then systematically applying the intrinsic or extrinsic rewards on a contingent basis when the desired outcome is achieved.

(TE/F.2) Review Training Content and Learned Skills

Research studies of memory (retention) following learning strongly indicate a sharp drop-off in recall capabilities following initial input. This decline is even worse when other factors interfere with immediate and regular application of the knowledge, or when significant time passes before the individual reviews the material. In short, everything points in the direction of the desirability of *early and frequent review*.

Trainees should establish a regular time for periodically reviewing their course materials following training. For example, during training some trainees commit themselves to return to the course manual and spend a half hour scanning the highlights at least once each month for a six-month period. Others create a "tickler file" with several copies of their previously created action plans; this automatically reminds them of the intentions they stated following training and helps to renew their commitment to change. The same process can be used with the contract for change that they may have initiated with their supervisor.

Another, more convenient option is frequent reference to job performance aids that the trainer (or supervisor) provided to stimulate better retention of knowledge and skills. The key is to recognize that memory loss will occur without a conscious intervention program, and then to use one or more methods to prevent or diminish that loss.

(TE/F.3) Develop a Mentoring Relationship

Relatively new in organizations, mentoring programs formally or informally match senior (experienced and successful) employees with other (newer) employees. Most formal mentoring programs have involved senior and junior managers. The purpose is to provide useful job and career guidance to the employees (protégés), as well as useful advice on mistakes to avoid and skills to develop. Mentors can also be available for job and personal counseling when needed and can aid an employee's career by serving as an advocate when the opportunity arises. Mentors from the same cultural background as trainees can provide particularly valuable assistance. In general, mentors are a rich potential source of useful information and guidance if used properly.

Trainees may find it useful to report back not only to their direct supervisors but also to their mentors following training. They can use the mentor as a source of feedback, aggressively bouncing new ideas off the mentor and asking for candid advice on the merits of using new approaches. They can also solicit feedback on the mentor's perceptions of actual change by the trainee. This constructive criticism by the mentor can be tremendously useful as a supplement to that obtained more formally from the direct supervisor.

(TE/F.4) Maintain Contact with Training "Buddies"

In Chapter 6 we recommended that trainees establish contact with one or more other trainees and develop a "buddy" relationship while still learning. Once trainees return to their jobs, it is easy for contact with buddies to lapse, especially if they are geographically separated or if they work in different units of the same company. As is true of many casual relationships, buddy relationships will deteriorate rapidly unless they are actively nurtured.

We advise trainees to commit publicly to a behavior change by announcing it (preferably in writing) to their buddies. Then it is imperative that regular follow-up contacts be negotiated and followed. For example, the buddies might agree to call one another on the last Friday of each month, with each partner taking responsibility in alternate months for initiating the call. They may agree to meet for lunch or after work on a regular basis, with an agenda of sharing their successful and less-successful efforts to implement what they learned, and then setting new behavioral goals.

The buddy's partner should be encouraged in advance to ask penetrating questions designed to discover how the buddy is actually doing. "Which items from our program have you used so far (or this month)? Which ones did you consciously consider but decide not to try, and why? What problems did you encounter when you tried to transfer a skill? What kind of support are you receiving for your effort? Have you had an opportunity to implement Idea A yet, as you promised to try last time? What are your plans for the next month? What can I do to help support your efforts?"

The entire purpose of the buddy relationship is to increase the likelihood of transfer through the use of interpersonal commitment, mutual support, goal setting, and the availability of an ally who has experienced the same process and can speak the same (sometimes technical, or at least unique) language. It also provides a safe alternative to the more formal conversations that might occur between trainees and their supervisors, thus leading to a more candid exchange. In our experience the key lies in the strength of the two parties' commitment to maintaining mutual contacts for an extended period.

The buddies must agree in advance that they will not allow their meetings to become merely an opportunity to complain to each other about how much work they have, how difficult it is to transfer new ideas, how unsupportive their colleagues are, and so on. Sharing the negatives in their situations is important, of course, to help each realize that he or she is not alone in facing problems. If the negatives can be kept in perspective, however, buddy relationships can become powerful transfer devices for following up on training efforts.

SUMMARY

A proverb suggests that even people's best-laid plans often go awry. The same can be said for much of today's training; good training never gets used, or not for very long. Even though managers, trainees, and trainers may have taken numerous actions before and during training to help cue and initiate transfer of training, it still invariably requires follow-up actions after training. This chapter has summarized a wide variety of posttraining strategies by managers, trainers, and trainees that can have a positive impact on successful transfer.

Major strategies include establishing mechanisms for review and refreshers, cueing high but reasonable expectations, making available (and using) reminder devices and job aids, providing opportunities for application, removing obstacles to transfer, making culturally-sensitive role models available, and offering positive reinforcement for successful progress. Collectively these provide a rich "tool kit" that managers, trainers, and trainees can use to improve transfer once the trainee returns to the job.

References

Byham, William C., Diane Adams, and Ann Kiggins. "Transfer of Modeling Training to the Job." *Personnel Psychology* 29 (1976): 345–49.

Fleishman, Edwin A., Edwin F. Harris, and Harold E. Burtt. *Leadership and Supervision in Industry.* Monograph no. 33. Columbus: Personnel Research Board, Ohio State University, 1955.

Lawler, Edward E. *High-Involvement Management: Participative Strategies for Improving Organizational Performance.* San Francisco: Jossey-Bass, 1986.

McLagan, Patricia S. "Top Management Support." *Training* (May 1988): 59–62.

Newstrom, John W., and Mark Lengnick-Hall. "One Size Does Not Fit All," *Training and Development Journal* (June 1991): 43–48.

Peters, Tom. *Thriving on Chaos: Handbook for a Management Revolution.* New York: Alfred A. Knopf, 1987.

Vroom, Victor H., and Arthur G. Jago. *The New Leadership: Managing Participation in Organizations.* Englewood Cliffs, N.J.: Prentice-Hall, 1988.

Chapter 8

RELAPSE PREVENTION: A SPECIAL ACTION-PLANNING STRATEGY DURING TRAINING

For many, the skills so carefully shaped during training do not survive the transition to the workplace. . . . The manager trained in relapse prevention re-enters the workplace as if it were a minefield capable of blowing good intentions to smithereens at one false step. Relapse prevention training is the mine detector.

— Robert D. Marx, "Self-Managed Skill Retention" (pp. 54, 55).

KEY THEMES FOR THIS CHAPTER:

• Special needs for transfer support: an unsupportive work environment
• The relapse prevention process
  —As a training program module
  —As a continuing resource

Chapters 5–7 described transfer strategies that are used before, during, and after training by the manager, trainer, and trainee. These strategies demonstrate management's support for the training effort, give the trainer greater impact on transfer, and provide tools for trainees to support transfer back on the job. Many of these strategies assume an encouraging supervisor and supportive work setting.

In this chapter we will look at a special situation, in which the job environment provides little built-in support for the trainee's new skills. We will explore a process by which trainees can take charge of the transfer process, anticipate barriers in difficult work situations, and plan how to find and maintain the support they need to transfer their learning successfully.

SPECIAL NEEDS FOR SUPPORT FOR TRANSFER BACK ON THE JOB

Some training situations require special attention to the challenges faced by trainees as they try to transfer their learning effectively to the job. In general these are situations in which the work environment is likely to be unsupportive, or even hostile, to the trainee's new learning.

For example, new supervisors may receive training in "effective listening" as a way to cope with emotional statements by employees. The training objective is for supervisors to reflect both the feelings and the content they hear the employee express. They learn to say something like, "What I hear you saying is that you are unhappy about the new work schedule, and you want to renegotiate your shift assignment," before reacting to the employee's statement. The goal is to verify both the content and the feeling conveyed by the employee before responding. This helps supervisors avoid responses based on inaccurate assumptions about what the employee wants to convey.

During training, the trainee (the new supervisor) may become relatively adept at responding in this style during various practice situations such as role plays. The trainee learns the value of checking what the speaker intended to communicate before possibly adding to the problem by a response based on misperceptions.

However, both the trainees and the trainer in the effective listening program recognize that this style of response may seem awkward and even evasive to employees in the culture of the work environment. The supervisor/trainee's manager also may not be familiar with this communication style and its purpose. Finally, the supervisor/trainee may find the response style very uncomfortable and feel the need for lots of practice and support back on the job if she is to build the new skill into her natural communication processes. Given these problems, it will be difficult for the new supervisor to start and continue to use these effective listening skills on the job.

There are, unfortunately, many work environments in which support for new skills may be absent. The trainees may be sales personnel who spend most of their time on the road, operating almost completely on their own without contact with supportive supervisors or co-workers. The manager of a division may be trying to introduce greater employee participation in decision making. An entire organization may be trying to change its culture from the traditional "power at the top, just do what the boss says," to employee empowerment; however, both managers and employees may be unused to (and possibly distrustful of) new patterns of communication and responsibility.

A creative approach to solving this type of problem has been developed by Robert Marx. He examined the relapse prevention efforts that have been built into various drug-abuse and alcohol-abuse programs. These relapse prevention sessions help "graduates" who have undergone significant behavior change during the programs to prepare to return to the immensely hostile and unsupportive environment in which their substance abuse problem originated.

Marx saw the relevance of the relapse prevention approach to management training situations in which the trainees, with new but unpracticed skills, return to an unsupportive work environment. The process he recommends, however, is applicable to many types of training in which trainees return to neutral or even hostile job situations. How can trainees be supported, against these odds, in applying new skills on the job and practicing until the skills can be used relatively easily? How can the trainee—in any type of training situation—be helped to avoid a relapse to reliance on easier (though less effective) pretraining behaviors?

The solution Marx developed was to include a *relapse prevention module* as one of the last sessions in the training program. In this session trainees are helped to look for relapse indicators in their own job situations and then to develop a plan to prevent their own relapse to old habits.

In an organization in which managers and trainers work together through the seven key performance improvement decisions described in Chapter 3, the possible need for a relapse prevention module will be addressed as the fourth decision is made (selecting training as part of the solution). Also, when managers, trainers, and trainees join in a Transfer Partnership, the need for such a module will be explored during the advance planning for training. If these partners find that one or more of the relapse indicators (to be described later) are present in the work situation, they can make sure a relapse prevention module is built into the training design.

RELAPSE INDICATORS

As a first step, Marx identified five factors in the work environment which suggest that the returning trainee may be vulnerable to relapse.

(1) There is a *backlog of work* which the trainee must handle quickly. Because pretraining behaviors are the easiest and quickest to use, the pressure of work may lead to relapse. (Paradoxically, lack of work and resulting boredom may also invite relapse.)

(2) *Co-workers do not support* the new behaviors and may urge the trainee to revert to former practices.

(3) *Other pressures*—such as reorganization, merger, multicultural differences, or personal problems—distract the trainee from giving time and attention to practicing new learning.

(4) The trainee may be *doubtful of his or her ability* to use new skills effectively.

(5) There may be *little or no management support* for use of new skills.

THE RELAPSE PREVENTION PROCESS

ADVANCE PLANNING

When one or more of Indicators 1 through 4 are present in the work environment, trainers and supportive managers should consider building a relapse prevention module into the training program. (If the fifth indicator is a factor, trainers and interested managers should reconsider whether training should be attempted at all until more management support is evident.)

When relapse is a real possibility, the trainer should initiate a Transfer Partnership at the earliest possible stage, contacting any managers and trainees who recognize and are concerned about the problem. They should discuss the relapse indicators and then select and implement any transfer strategies, before and during training, which fit the organizational situation. They should also plan and design a relapse prevention module and make sure that the relapse problem—and the roles of *all partners* in its solution—are acknowledged throughout the program.

RELAPSE PREVENTION MODULE

The relapse prevention module is usually included near the end of the training program. During the initial part of the relapse prevention module, trainees do a final analysis of their work environment to identify all possible relapse indicators. In small groups, they help each other probe for evidence of those indicators and discuss each indicator in detail. If appropriate, and if possible, managers and co-workers of trainees can be included throughout the entire module.

Next, trainees work through the five-step relapse prevention process (see Figure 8.1) and apply each step to their own situation. Small- and large-group discussions allow trainees to get the benefit of ideas from all participants.

Figure 8.1   RELAPSE PREVENTION PROCESS

1. Recognize that *lapses are inevitable*
   - Provide data for future improvement
   - Note evidence of inadequacy

2. Identify *predictable problem areas* related to *relapse indicators*
   - Work backlog back on the job
   - Unsupportive co-workers
   - Other pressures
   - Doubts of own ability to use skills
   - No management support

3. Analyze available *coping skills*
   - Managing time effectively
   - Communicating clearly
   - Setting priorities
   - Collecting data
   - Avoiding self-blame
   - Developing allies
   - Celebrating accomplishments

4. Plan and conduct *fire drills*
   - Times and situations in which lapses are likely
   - Available supportive resources
   - Strategies to keep a lapse from becoming a relapse

5. *Follow-up* back on the job
   - Individual learner tracks *accomplishments*
   - Groups of learners provide *mutual support*
   - Trainer provides *encouragement* and *coaching*
   - Manager provides *encouragement* and *reinforcement*

Summarized from Marx (1983).

Step 1. Recognize that Lapses Are Inevitable

The discussion of lapses—falling back on previous, less effective habits instead of trying newly learned behaviors—emphasizes two points:

- *A lapse is not evidence of inadequacy or failure.* Trainees are human, and lapses are to be expected—particularly when trainees are under stress while trying to unlearn long-standing habits and move to new behaviors.

- *A lapse provides very useful information* about the situations trainees should watch out for. Each lapse gives clues and reminders for pitfalls to avoid and directions for future improvement. Trainees might keep a "lapse log" to capture this important information.

In our earlier example, the new supervisor may be confronted by an employee with a problem on the first day back on the job, and may forget to say, "What I hear you say is . . . " The supervisor may realize shortly that she has slipped and be unhappy that she didn't perform effectively at the first opportunity. However, her relapse prevention planning should help the supervisor recognize that a lapse is not an indicator of total or permanent failure. She can analyze the lapse situation to identify probable future pitfalls. The training will help the supervisor to remain optimistic and encourage her to try again when the next chance occurs.

Step 2. Identify Predictable Problem Areas for the Future

Next, trainees review the relapse indicators they have identified and brainstorm the types of situations that might call for use of the new skills in a typical work day. For each situation, they consider (and take notes on) all aspects that might make it difficult to use the skills effectively.

To pursue our example, the newly trained supervisor may have one employee who is particularly difficult to deal with—a person who has a habit of challenging authority. During the relapse prevention session, the supervisor imagines different scenarios in which this employee might confront her, and in which she (the supervisor) would want to use her new effective listening skills. She makes notes on each possible scenario: the issue, the setting, the time of day, and so on. Similarly, she analyzes and makes notes on situations with other employees which would call for use of the new skills.

Step 3. Analyze Available Resources and Coping Skills

Trainees now analyze all possible external resources that could help them begin to use new skills effectively. For our example, external resources might include job aids (wall charts or pocket cards listing examples of effective listening statements) and audiotapes on effective listening for the new supervisor to play during her drive to work. For other new skills, external resources might include regular reports, software programs, and organizational policies and practices.

Next, the trainee identifies coping skills that can help her use new behaviors more effectively when she returns to the job. As Figure 8.1 suggests, the supervisor/trainee can *manage her time more efficiently* so that she has time to practice new skills. She can *set more realistic work priorities* to focus on high-priority projects without becoming overwhelmed and vulnerable to lapses.

A particularly important coping skill is to *identify allies* to provide support for transfer. These might be co-workers who previously had the same training, a sympathetic supervisor or mentor, or the trainer who presented the effective listening program. The supervisor can consciously provide her own reinforcement by *celebrating any success in using new skills*. Finally, she can *avoid self-blame when lapses occur*.

Step 4. Plan and Conduct "Fire Drills"

During the session each trainee focuses on a particular situation in which lapse is likely and identifies available supportive resources. He or she develops a scenario demonstrating use of the new skills and strategies to keep a lapse (if one should occur) from becoming a relapse to old behaviors. Then trainees help each other role-play each situation to practice skills and strategies.

The supervisor in our example describes a typical challenge from her difficult employee. Another trainee then role-plays the employee while the supervisor/trainee practices effective listening techniques and steps to recover from a lapse. A third trainee acts as the observer, providing feedback and coaching to the supervisor. Finally, the whole group discusses common problems and helpful techniques. These "fire drills" help to prepare the trainee for real work situations soon to come.

Step 5. Follow-Up Back on the Job

The final step in the relapse prevention module is for trainees to plan how they will keep track of their accomplishments and what reinforcement they will seek for their successes. The trainees' managers and co-workers, if present, can be particularly helpful in planning their contributions back on the job.

The supervisor in our example decides to keep a log of all instances in which she tries to use effective listening skills and to note how successful she is. She will also record each time she lapses and forgets to use the skills. She promises herself that the first time she successfully uses effective listening skills with her difficult employee, she will reward herself.

After returning to the job, groups of trainees might get together to provide mutual support. Supervisors and/or trainees might arrange for the trainer to give a follow-up session or ongoing coaching on the job. Supportive supervisors can provide recognition or other reinforcement, tailored to the individual trainee, for success in transferring new skills.

RELAPSE PREVENTION: A CONTINUING RESOURCE

The relapse prevention process can be a useful resource in many situations long after its first use as a module in a training program. Supervisors and subordinates can work through each step of the process in informal planning sessions whenever they want to provide structured support for transferring new skills to the job. Groups of employees can use the process at any time to plan and carry out changes in work relationships or procedures.

The relapse prevention process can also be a genuine resource to readers of this book. Trainers can adapt the five-step process to plan and implement a move into the role of manager of transfer of training for the organization. We will return to this suggestion in Chapter 10.

SUMMARY

The relapse prevention process should be part of the design of a training program whenever relapse indicators are present in the trainee's work situation. The process helps trainees to identify potential problems, plan how to deal with them, and practice coping strategies. Any support that managers, co-workers, mentors, or others can provide will help relapse prevention become a viable and constructive tool for change in the organization.

This completes our detailed discussion of a wide range of strategies to support transfer of training to the job. In previous chapters we have presented a rich menu of strategies to support transfer of training before, during, and after training takes place. This chapter has focused on particularly unsupportive work environments and suggested inclusion of a relapse prevention module in the training program. The goal of the following chapters is to "put it all together" by showing some examples of transfer management in action, and by proposing processes to help trainers move into the role of manager of transfer in their organizations.

References

Marx, Robert D. "Relapse Prevention for Managerial Training: A Model for Maintenance of Behavior Change." *Academy of Management Review* (July 1982): 433–441.

————. "Relapse Prevention in Management Education." In *Proceedings of the Academy of Management Annual Meeting*, Dallas, Tx., August 1983.

————. "Relapse Prevention in Management Training: Self-Control Strategies for Skill Retention." In *Proceedings of the American Psychological Association Annual Meeting,* Toronto, Ontario, August 1984.

————. "Self-Managed Skill Retention." *Training and Development Journal* (January 1986): 54–57.

Part III

USING AND SUPPORTING TRANSFER IN THE ORGANIZATION

Chapter 9

MANAGING TRANSFER OF TRAINING: APPLICATIONS IN ORGANIZATIONS

The training/HRD/performance improvement professional—with the greatest transfer expertise—[has] a unique opportunity to move into a new and more powerful role in the organization, as manager of the transfer process.
— Mary L. Broad, "Transfer of Training" (p. 108).

KEY THEME FOR THIS CHAPTER:

• Transfer management in action: the trainer as manager of transfer for the organization
—Yellow Freight System
—Hughes Training, Inc.

This chapter looks at two examples of transfer management in organizational settings. In each case trainers and managers recognized from the start the need to work together to ensure that the investment in training paid off in full and continuing transfer of new knowledge and skills to the job. In both situations trainers played the role we consider to be of primary importance in organizations today—manager of transfer—to initiate and oversee the transfer support effort.

In these examples we will review the key performance improvement decisions in order and the important considerations for each (as described in Chapter 3). We will look at barriers to transfer, formation of the Transfer Partnership, and transfer strategies that were used. A basic theme throughout is the trainer's new role as *manager of transfer of training.*

YELLOW FREIGHT SYSTEM

The first example, at Yellow Freight System, is described in the literature by Jack Zigon and Bob Cicerone (1986) and by Zigon (1986). The project involved a comprehensive, systemwide attempt to improve the performance of management personnel in a large transportation firm of 21,000 employees. The project was directed by Zigon, then manager of the organization's Human Resource Development Department (and now president of Zigon Performance Group).

This is the best-documented published example we have found of the training function taking on the role of manager of transfer: working closely with the organization's top management to make key performance improvement decisions, to form the Transfer Partnership, and to plan and implement a wide range of strategies to support transfer to the job. In the literature the project is described in terms of Thomas Gilbert's *performance engineering* model (1978). In our discussion we translate the project's application of that model into our model of managers and trainers sharing key performance improvement decisions, forming the Transfer Partnership, and applying strategies by managers, trainers, and trainees before, during, and after training takes place.

KEY DECISIONS ON PERFORMANCE IMPROVEMENT

(1) *Identify the need for performance improvement.* Shortly after being established in 1981, the HRD Department at Yellow Freight undertook a systemwide needs analysis. Interviews were conducted with top managers, resulting in identification of three groups of employees whose performance needed improvement: branch managers, sales representatives, and front-line supervisors. Further analysis identified the gap between exemplary and average performance in each category and focused on branch managers as the group with the potential for greatest return on investment in training.

(2) *Identify the probable causes of the performance problem/opportunity.* Several causes were identified for the performance problems of branch managers. Although higher-level managers had clear performance measures and standards, employees below the branch manager level did not. Performance feedback was not consistently given to individual employees by branch managers. There was no formal reward system for lower-level employees, other than retaining their jobs. Training for lower-level employees was unstructured and unsystematic.

(3) *Address work environment and motivational causes for the performance problem/opportunity.* The HRD Department recommended that the organization's performance management system be improved by developing per-

formance standards, feedback systems, and rewards for all jobs. The recommendations were accepted and implemented.

(4) *When the need for additional knowledge or skill is a significant cause of
the performance problem/opportunity, consider training as part of the solution.*
The branch managers had to learn how to use the improved performance
management system. Specifically, they had to learn how to develop performance standards for each job, gain agreement from employees on the standards, provide feedback on performance, work with employees to resolve
performance problems, and provide appropriate rewards. The HRD Department recommended training in these skills for all branch managers and for
higher-level managers who supervise them. Top management accepted this
recommendation.

(5) *Develop the Transfer Partnership and implement transfer strategies* (in
conjunction with Decision 6). Top-level managers and the HRD Department
worked as partners throughout the project; trainees were not brought in as
partners until they entered the training program. Specific transfer strategies
used are described below.

Before training, by the manager:

M/B.1:   *Build transfer of training into supervisory performance stan-
          dards.* Top managers directed that a standard, "Employees'
          Performance Managed"—including support for transfer—
          be incorporated into all managers' performance standards.

M/B.3:   *Involve supervisors and trainees in needs analysis procedures.*
          Chairman of the board, president, vice presidents, and area
          managers were involved in the needs analysis. (Trainees
          were not involved at this stage.)

M/B.6:   *Brief trainees on the importance of the training and on course
          objectives, content, process, and application to the job.* Top
          managers (chairman of the board and vice presidents) pre-
          pared a videotape, which was played at the start of each
          workshop session. In the tape the chairman emphasized the
          need for the program and his personal support; the vice
          presidents stated that they had been through the program,
          intended to use the skills, and expected all managers to use
          them as well. A personal letter to each trainee from the
          chairman at the start of the program emphasized strong

management support. An employee newsletter article gave a preview of content and examples of job aids used in the program.

M/B.7:   *Review instructional content and materials.* Selected managers reviewed content and materials in advance and received recognition for their participation.

M/B.13:   *Send co-workers to training together.* The HRD Department was funded to cover all trainee expenses, rather than charge them back to organizational components, so managers were free to send trainees to the program without financial constraints.

M/B.15:   *Plan to participate in training sessions.* From vice presidents down, each level of management participated in and demonstrated use of the skills. Managers who applied the skills well served as trainers for many of the workshop presentations; as trainers they received a variety of rewards: a promotion and raise in pay as they started their tour as trainers and additional promotions after the tour ended.

Before training, by the trainer:

TR/B.3:   *Systematically design instruction.* The training was designed following a systematic instructional systems design process (see Decision 6).

TR/B.4:   *Provide practice opportunities.* Practice opportunities were built into the program for all objectives (see Decision 6).

During training, by the manager:

M/D.3:   *Communicate supervisory/managerial support for the program.* The videotape of top managers supporting the program was played at the start of each workshop. The monthly employee newsletter presented a regular story on the program, including numbers trained, management support, and examples of successes by managers using the skills.

M/D.5:   *Recognize trainee participation.* Trainees who successfully completed the program were recognized and received certificates signed by the chairman of the board and a vice president.

During training, by the trainer:

TR/D.1:   *Develop application-oriented objectives.* The training objectives focused on how trainees would apply the new skills on the job.

TR/D.4:   *Provide realistic work-related tasks.* Trainees were provided with samples of job models and feedback reports, which were used as examples during training.

TR/D.6:   *Give individualized feedback.* Trainers provided feedback (with lots of positive reinforcement) to trainees on their performance during exercises and videotaped practice sessions.

TR/D.7:   *Provide job performance aids.* Job aids were designed to be used during training, to learn new skills, and after training to support effective performance on the job.

During training, by the trainee:

TE/D.7:   *Create behavioral contracts.* At the close of the workshop the trainees developed contracts specifying how they would apply the new skills in their work situation.

Following training, by the manager:

M/F.8:   *Give positive reinforcement.* Back on the job, the trainees' supervisors gave feedback and positive reinforcement on use of the new skills. Each trainee's vice president sent a personal letter giving congratulations on successful application of new skills.

M/F.9:   *Provide role models.* Supervisors of trainees had been trained to demonstrate the new skills and encourage their use by trainees.

Following training, by the trainer:

TR/F.2:   *Provide follow-up support.* Trainers followed up with each trainee to give support and feedback on their use of new skills.

TR/F.3:   *Conduct evaluation surveys and provide feedback.* The HRD Department developed monthly reports for top management on the status of the project. HRD staff conducted a comprehen-

sive evaluation of the project's accomplishments, through follow-up interviews with trainees several months after their
return to the job, and were able to demonstrate significant
performance improvement and large dollar cost savings.

TR/F.4:   *Develop and administer recognition systems.* The HRD Department gave awards to all trainees who used the new skills
and publicized their successes and positive comments about
the training program in the monthly newsletter.

(6) *Design and deliver training* (in conjunction with Decision 5). There
were two major performance objectives for the program. The trainees should
be able to demonstrate the performance management skills (creating job
models and feedback systems, trouble-shooting employee performance
problems, and rewarding employees). They should also be able to demonstrate necessary "people" skills: interpersonal skills, communicating expectations, and coaching to improve employee performance. The program was
designed following a systematic instructional systems design process and included many practice and demonstration opportunities; it was presented to
more than 1,000 managers.

(7) *Evaluate training outcomes.* The HRD Department evaluated the program on four dimensions.

Trainee reactions: The more than 1,000 trainees rated the use and relevance of the program an average of 4.9 on a five-point Likert scale.

Trainee learning: 99.7% of the trainees successfully completed the program by passing at least 8 of 10 criterion tests.

Behavior on the job: 88% of the trainees provided evidence, in follow-up
surveys, that they were maintaining use of the new skills in the work
environment.

Results: The estimated value of performance improvements resulting
from the training was more than $20 million.

COMMENTS ON TRANSFER MANAGEMENT AT YELLOW FREIGHT

It is an axiom that we restate frequently: all organizational settings and all training situations are different; no single transfer process is best for all. Our comments on Yellow Freight's transfer management process will reflect that caution.

First, Yellow Freight's HRD Department trainers acted as full partners with management through all the key decisions. They were recognized by the organization as managers of the entire transfer process.

The Transfer Partnership for this program included trainers (HRD Department members and managers who served as temporary trainers) and managers (supervisors and managers of trainees). Trainees were not significantly involved in transfer strategies before or after training (although there may have been more involvement than is mentioned in published descriptions of this project). However, their level of involvement seemed to be sufficient to make the project a success.

The project developers did not focus explicitly on barriers to transfer of training. However, the transfer strategies they selected show a wish to avoid certain barriers: lack of reinforcement on the job, trainees' discomfort with change, and separation from the trainer. When a new system (performance, hardware, and/or software) is being installed, it is often useful to focus on supportive transfer strategies rather than on negatives of potential barriers.

The Yellow Freight example demonstrates an important point: use of a variety of transfer strategies is highly recommended. They used 20 in this project (although several overlap, depending on the role or time frame). Until we have a sufficient body of research to pinpoint exactly which strategies are effective in specific situations, reliance on one or two strategies will be ineffective. Clearly the trainers and managers involved in the Yellow Freight program were convinced that multiple transfer strategies paid off.

HUGHES TRAINING, INC.

In 1990 Hughes Training, Inc. (then Flight Simulation Operations), had approximately 320 employees producing sophisticated flight simulators, almost exclusively for the U.S. Department of Defense. The organization, a subsidiary of Hughes Aircraft, has a matrix management structure, primarily organized by product area and cross-organized by function. Kay Quam, manager of Human Resources, and Dr. Mary Lippitt, president of Enterprise Management, Ltd., worked together to provide training for managers and supervisors.

Both the human resources manager and the consultant were strong proponents of designing training for use on the job. The vice president for the operation also required that the training investment have a direct payoff on the job. Dr. Lippitt, the trainer, was familiar with the authors' Transfer Partnership model—managers, trainers, and trainees working together, using multiple strategies to support transfer before, during, and after training. As in our earlier example, we will review key decisions on performance improvement, formation of the Transfer Partnership, and use of transfer strategies. Again, we will translate this project's procedures and events into our model's terms.

KEY DECISIONS ON PERFORMANCE IMPROVEMENT

(1) *Identify the need for performance improvement.* Hughes Training, Inc., was shifting from reliance on Defense Department contracts to a wider government sector focus. The human resources manager recognized that an effective matrix organization undergoing such a transition demands a high degree of cross-functional coordination. To increase operational effectiveness and efficiency, she proposed a focus on improving communications, developing problem-solving abilities, and building an organization-wide perspective.

(2) *Identify the probable causes of the performance problem/opportunity.* Managers and supervisors, who had to integrate experts in several disciplines in their projects, were not persuasive in their communication and problem-solving interactions with their direct reports or with their peers.

(3) *Address work environment and motivational causes for the performance problem/opportunity.* Top management recognized that current organizational structures and practices should be examined to ensure that planning and coordination among program and functional managers were effective. After several months of analysis and planning for change, the organization was restructured in early 1991 to facilitate collaboration.

(4) *When the need for additional knowledge or skill is a significant cause of the performance problem/opportunity, consider training as part of the solution.* The human resources manager and the training consultant recommended, and the vice president approved, training for managers and supervisors in persuasive communication techniques (e.g., negotiation, communications strategies) to support cross-departmental collaboration. An additional learning requirement, identified during preliminary conferences with trainees and their managers, was interdepartmental coordination of projects.

(5) *Develop the Transfer Partnership and implement transfer strategies* (in conjunction with Decision 6). The human resources manager and the trainer worked closely with the operation's vice president and managers throughout the project. Trainees were involved as part of the Transfer Partnership to contribute to the needs analysis in the project's early stages. Specific transfer strategies which were used in this project included the following.

Before training, by the manager:

M/B.3: *Involve supervisors and trainees in needs analysis procedures.* The human resources manager and consultant trainer met with the vice president and senior managers to identify performance improvement needs, organizational priorities, and issues or outcomes that should be avoided. (Trainees were involved after initial needs were identified; see M/B.5.)

M/B.4: *Provide orientations for supervisors.* A preview of the program's objectives and content was provided to the vice president and senior managers.

M/B.5: *Involve trainees in program planning.* Focus groups, including about half of the trainees, met with the trainer to discuss training needs, the program's design, their interests and expectations, and the prework project. They were encouraged to bring work-related issues to the course.

M/B.6: *Brief trainees on the importance of the training and on course objectives, content, process, and application to the job.* All trainees received invitations from their managers describing the training and its importance to the organization.

M/B.7: *Review instructional content and materials.* The trainer met with selected trainee managers to discuss content. These managers also developed real-life cases for the program using a model provided by the trainer.

M/B.9: *Provide time to complete precourse assignments.* Prework was distributed one or two weeks in advance of training; this was considered part of the trainee's work assignments.

M/B.13: *Send co-workers to training together.* About 50 trainees (80% of all managers and supervisors) attended two presentations of the three-day course.

M/B.14: *Provide a positive training environment (timing, location, facilities).* The off-site facility was first-class, with continental breakfast and lunch provided.

M/B.15: *Plan to participate in training sessions.* The vice president and senior managers made commitments to attend the kickoff and closing sessions of the program and to participate in the follow-up sessions.

Before training, by the trainer:

TR/B.1:   *Align the HRD program with the organization's strategic plan.* Preliminary conferences with the vice president ensured that the program fit the organization's strategic direction.

TR/B.2:   *Involve managers and trainees.* Trainees and their managers were involved in preliminary meetings with the trainer to assess needs and discuss issues and concerns. Managers helped to develop case materials for use in the program.

TR/B.3:   *Systematically design instruction.* The trainer followed a systematic instructional design process.

TR/B.4:   *Provide practice opportunities.* Trainees brought real job issues to be worked on as class projects and practiced negotiation skills with the customized case studies developed by the managers.

TR/B.5:   *Develop trainee readiness.* Pretraining conferences and prework prepared trainees for the program's content and approach.

Before training, by the trainees:

TE/B.1:   *Provide input into program planning.* In preliminary meetings trainees contributed to the program's objectives and design.

TE/B.3:   *Participate in advance activities.* Trainees attended pretraining conferences and completed prework in advance of the program.

During training, by the manager:

M/D.1:   *Prevent interruptions.* The off-site location minimized work-related interruptions.

M/D.3:   *Communicate supervisory/managerial support for the program.* The vice president and top managers participated in the program's opening, closing, and follow-up sessions. Managers took the same self-assessment instruments as a basis for later conferences with participants.

M/D.5:   *Recognize trainee participation.* At the closing session the top managers expressed satisfaction and support for trainees' accomplishments.

M/D.6:   *Participate in transfer action planning.* At the closing session senior managers announced follow-up sessions for project participants and a follow-up session with the vice president on the status of projects.

During training, by the trainer:

TR/D.1:   ˜*Develop application-oriented objectives.* All program objectives (communication strategies, problem solving, organization-wide understanding, and project implementation) were oriented to on-the-job application.

TR/D.2:   *Manage the unlearning process.* During the program trainees assessed themselves on management skills and discussed how the program's objectives would help them manage more effectively.

TR/D.3:   *Answer the "WIIFM" question.* Trainees saw the program as a means to resolve technical problems, communicate with upper-level management, meet deadlines, and increase turnaround speed. They welcomed the chance to address real issues, build relationships with peers, and become informed on departmental systems.

TR/D.4:   *Provide realistic work-related tasks.* The case examples prepared by managers, and trainees' own work projects, were subjects of program exercises.

TR/D.6:   *Give individualized feedback.* The trainer provided (to those who requested it) individualized feedback on communication strengths and challenges. Trainee volunteers made individual practice presentations and received group feedback.

TR/D.9:   *Create opportunities for support groups.* Several project groups continued after training was completed, with support from department managers and the human resources manager.

TR/D.10:   *Help trainees prepare group action plans.* Project teams prepared action plans for continued work on their projects and status reports at later follow-up sessions.

TR/D.12:   *Design and conduct relapse prevention sessions.* The trainer worked with trainees to identify barriers that would block transfer and specific transfer strategies (by managers, trainer, and trainees themselves) that would support transfer and maintenance of their new skills and knowledge.

During training, by the trainee:

TE/D.3:   *Participate actively.* Trainees worked actively on meaningful projects during the program.

TE/D.5:   *Plan for applications.* Trainees worked on specific skills and projects that would be used on the job. For example, each developed a strategy for a difficult communication challenge on the job.

TE/D.6:   *Anticipate relapse.* Participants identified barriers to their transfer of new learning and specified the transfer strategies (by managers, trainer, and themselves) that would support transfer.

Following training, by the manager:

M/F.4:   *Provide opportunities to practice new skills.* Trainees were encouraged by top managers to apply new skills in projects and meetings immediately back on the job. Follow-up sessions and a project status report meeting with the vice president were scheduled.

M/F.5:   *Have trainees participate in transfer-related decisions.* Participants selected the projects they would work on during and after training.

M/F.7:   *Debrief the trainer.* Top managers and the human resources manager discussed the program's outcomes with the trainer shortly after the program ended.

M/F.8:   *Give positive reinforcement.* At the follow-up status meeting the vice president commended project leaders. Then, and in later meetings, he referred often to the positive results of the program.

M/F.14:   *Support trainee reunions.* The trainer was invited back to a follow-up session with trainees and executives five weeks after the program ended.

M/F.15:   *Publicize successes.* The vice president gave recognition to the projects completed as a result of training and other projects stimulated by the training. Estimated savings to the organization were over $300,000 in the first six months following the program.

Following training, by the trainer:

TR/F.2:   *Provide follow-up support.* The human resources manager monitored the status of projects following the program. The trainer participated in a follow-up session five weeks after training was completed.

TR/F.3:   *Conduct evaluation surveys and provide feedback.* The trainer provided both a midcourse evaluation session, to consider possible changes in direction, and a final evaluation on the program's effectiveness and remaining needs for further development.

Following training, by the trainees:

TE/F.2:   *Review training content and learned skills.* Participants' continuing work on project teams provided ongoing opportunities to review content and practice new skills.

(6) *Design and deliver training* (in conjunction with Decision 5). The trainer designed an interactive, applications-oriented program based on input from managers, trainees, and the human resources manager. Learner objectives included developing and practicing communications skills (primarily listening and negotiating) to meet specific needs, assessing personal communication styles and developing strategies for dealing with other styles, and developing an individual plan to support increased organizational effectiveness. Approximately 50 employees participated in the training.

(7) *Evaluate training outcomes.* Participants rated the program as good to excellent. The organization's top managers expressed strong satisfaction with the results of projects and improvement in communications. The success of the program brought an increased commitment to training and contributed to establishment of an organization-wide quality improvement process.

COMMENTS ON TRANSFER MANAGEMENT AT HUGHES TRAINING, INC.

In this transfer example, as at Yellow Freight, the trainer (in this case an external consultant) worked as a full partner with the organization's management throughout the project. The human resources manager and the consultant trainer jointly functioned as managers of the transfer process. The human resources manager concentrated on oversight of internal transfer strategies, while the trainer focused on the program's design and integration into the organization.

The Transfer Partnership for this HRD program included managers at the top and middle levels and brought trainees in as full partners almost from the beginning of the process. Both trainees and managers provided input for the needs analysis and for the project's content, objectives, and design.

The trainer and the human resources manager used the Transfer Partnership model—managers, trainers, and trainees working together to identify and implement transfer strategies before, during, and after training. They drew on their common philosophy of respect for participants and systematic integrated approaches. Based on their experience, they planned for credibility of the program by emphasizing its utility and payoff to the organization in changed behaviors on the job. The selection of specific strategies and participants was based on knowledge of the organization's and employees' cultures and goals.

This example also demonstrates the value of using multiple transfer strategies. A total of 39 strategies was used (though, as in the earlier example, several are duplicates of the same strategy, from another role perspective). The managers, trainer, and human resources manager agree that effective use of transfer strategies was a major factor in the program's success.

SUMMARY

The foregoing examples described how trainers in two different organizations successfully initiated the Transfer Partnership and managed the transfer process. In both cases the trainers presented the rationale for emphasis on transfer to top managers in the organization and gained their support and involvement throughout the process. In one case trainees' full involvement began as the training program got under way; in the other trainees were brought in as full partners in the Transfer Partnership at the earliest stages of program design. In both situations multiple transfer strategies were used before, during, and after training. And in both situations managers credited the focus on transfer as a major factor in the successful outcomes of the training initiatives.

In the last chapter we present suggestions on how trainers can move into the three roles described earlier. The trainer becomes a strategic resource to the organization by linking HRD efforts to strategic goals and by sharing decisions on performance improvement with management. The trainer can be seen as an expert HRD resource by becoming more knowledgeable in HRD technologies and skills and by functioning as a skilled consultant to support organizational change. Finally, the trainer takes on the role of manager of the transfer process by advocating transfer to the organization, initiating Transfer Partnerships for major HRD programs, and managing the implementation of transfer strategies.

References

Broad, Mary L. "Transfer of Training: Building Manager/Trainer/Trainee Support into the Performance System." In *Performance Technology 1989: Selected Proceedings of the 27th NSPI Conference.* Denver, Colo.: National Society for Performance and Instruction, 1989: 98–109.

Gilbert, Thomas F. *Human Competence: Engineering Worthy Performance.* New York: McGraw-Hill, 1978.

Zigon, Jack. "Commentary: Change as a Performance to be Engineered." Chapter 18 in *Introduction to Performance Technology.* Washington, D.C.: National Society for Performance and Instruction, 1986.

Zigon, Jack, and Bob Cicerone. "Teaching Managers How to Improve Employee Performance." *Performance and Instruction Journal* (September 1986): 3–6.

Chapter 10

BUILDING AND MANAGING THE TRANSFER SYSTEM

These are difficult and challenging times for American companies. If we are going to survive them, we need the leadership of the training and development profession. Become agents of change within your organizations. Link your efforts to the strategic direction of your company. Training and development is coming of age. It is a function that is in the mainstream and is a competitive weapon for those companies who use it wisely.

— David T. Kearns, Chief Executive Officer, Xerox Corporation

KEY THEMES FOR THIS CHAPTER:

- Building credibility as a strategic and expert resource to the organization
- Forming the Transfer Partnership
- Gaining recognition as manager of transfer for the organization
- Developing an action plan to move into and maintain these roles

In earlier chapters we showed that much of the enormous investment in HRD in the United States is wasted, principally because training is not fully transferred to the work site. We looked at barriers to transfer and ways to address them, and emphasized that performance improvement decisions should be shared by managers and trainers for greatest impact. New roles have emerged for trainers: as strategic resources, linking HRD efforts to the organization's strategic goals and sharing in key performance improvement decisions, and as expert HRD resources, applying state-of-the art technologies to performance improvement challenges. A primary new role is manager of transfer (developing the Transfer Partnership and managing use of multiple transfer strategies). We presented almost 80 strategies—by managers, trainers, and trainees before, during, and after training—that support full transfer of training to the job.

In this final chapter we will help readers figure out "how to get there from here." Moving into the role of manager of transfer empowers the trainer to focus the organization's attention on the low payoff for training investments when transfer problems are ignored, major barriers, key performance improvement decisions, the Transfer Partnership, and transfer strategies.

This is good news for trainers. Everything necessary to focus the organization's attention on transfer is available to all who have read the previous chapters and who follow the recommendations of this chapter. These are presented on three levels: first, for the trainer who is just getting started in considering new roles; second, for those who have made some progress and want to continue moving forward; and third, for those who are already doing well in these roles. Based on their organizational situations, trainers can choose the steps that will most benefit them. These can then be incorporated into an individualized action plan for moving into these important roles.

No prescribed sequence for moving into these roles fits all situations. Some trainers are one-person shops; others are part of highly specialized HRD staffs in large organizations. We hope the steps we outline are generic enough to be adapted and applied widely. Moving forward on any of the steps is valuable. The savvy trainer will look for opportunities to take a parallel step, to fit a particular organizational setting.

ASSESSING ACCOMPLISHMENTS IN MOVING INTO NEW ROLES

Several indicators are benchmarks for measuring progress in gaining recognition in the roles of strategic resource, expert HRD resource, and manager of transfer (see Figure 3.3). These indicators are goals towards which trainers can move from current levels to the level they wish to attain.

To begin, we suggest you examine Figure 10.1. It presents a simple way to assess current levels of accomplishment by trainers in moving into new roles. The assessment form gives seven statements that are indicators of recognition in those roles. We have established three levels of accomplishment to determine, for each indicator, if the trainer is "getting started" (no efforts are under way but the trainer is interested), "moving forward" (some progress has been made), or "doing well" (significant progress has been made).

Figure 10.1 ASSESSING CURRENT LEVELS OF ACCOMPLISHMENT IN NEW TRAINER ROLES: STRATEGIC RESOURCE, EXPERT RESOURCE, AND MANAGER OF TRANSFER OF TRAINING

	No Action 0	Getting Started 1	Moving Forward 2	3	Doing Well 4	5

Strategic Resource

1. The trainer participates in the strategic planning process.

2. HRD programs are endorsed by management as supporting the strategic plan.

3. The trainer shares key performance improvement decisions with managers.

Expert Resource

4. The trainer is recognized as an HRD expert.

5. The trainer provides consulting skills for high-level organizational change efforts.

Manager of Transfer of Training

6. Managers, trainers, and trainees form an effective Transfer Partnership for each major HRD program.

7. The trainer is recognized as manager of transfer for the organization.

Scoring:

No Action: This is not a priority issue. (Zero points)
Getting Started: I'm interested in moving into new roles. (1 point)
Moving Forward: Some progress with at least one manager. (2–3 points)
Doing Well: Significant progress with several managers. (4–5 points)

Your total score: _____

Ratings:

   0 points: Return the book to the shelf; check again in another year.
 1–7 points: Good for you, you've started to move!
 8–21 points: Congratulations, you're gaining momentum!
22–35 points: Take pride in your accomplishments and keep moving!

The indicators are stated at the level of "doing well." After reading our discussion of each indicator, a firm "Yes, there is significant progress on this indicator with several managers!" merits an X in the "Doing Well" column and either four or five points. If the response is "No way, there's no hope in this organization!" the X should go in the "No Action" column; zero points. If the response is simply "I'm interested!" an X should go in the "Getting Started" column, for one point. For "Moving Forward" responses—between "Getting Started" and "Doing Well"—the trainer should mark either two or three points. As a rule of thumb, we suggest that a total score of 1–7 implies "getting started," a score of 8–21 points indicates "moving forward," and a score of 22–35 points means "doing well."

The levels of accomplishment for each indicator are *not* measures of the trainer's energy or competence. They are intended as measures of the organization's readiness to recognize HRD's strategic importance in achieving gains in productivity and competitiveness. The steps we propose will help the trainer to educate and encourage managers to support the HRD function in moving into these new roles.

As we discuss the indicators, we suggest that readers estimate (X) their accomplishment for each and, on another sheet of paper, jot down the evidence supporting their estimate for each indicator. This evidence will be important for discussing the assessment with managers and for building the action plan.

From this point on, our discussion assumes that the *trainer* is doing the analysis and developing the action plan. If the reader is a manager or trainee, we suggest that the next move is to get this book into the trainer's hands with a strong recommendation to read it promptly! Then work together to make the assessment and build an action plan.

All it takes for a minimum score on our assessment form is interest in moving into new roles and resolving transfer problems. Most trainers—and most organizations—have begun to recognize a few transfer problems and to address them in some fashion. Readers probably discovered several transfer strategies in Chapters 5 through 8 which their organizations have used. However, these efforts are often haphazard and uncoordinated.

As we outline the steps for trainers to move toward recognition in these new roles, readers who have already made progress on a particular indicator can find the point at which they can adapt new ideas to their organizational situations. All indicators and recommended steps are presented in Figure 10.2. Then, for each indicator, the story of Pat, head of the HRD function at Bestway Company, illustrates the steps we recommend at each level of accomplishment.

Figure 10.2   STEPS IN MOVING INTO NEW TRAINER ROLES:
STRATEGIC RESOURCE, EXPERT HRD RESOURCE,
AND MANAGER OF TRANSFER OF TRAINING

STRATEGIC RESOURCE

1. *Indicator:* The trainer participates in the strategic planning process.

Key Steps

1.1 Gather information on the organization's strategic planning process and on strategic planning by other organizations or associations in the industry.

1.2 Become familiar with the business of the organization, particularly the range and types of expertise necessary to produce products and services for both internal and external customers.

1.3 Get copies of organizational studies, reports, and analyses of the current workforce: skills, previous training, career development plans or guidelines, age, eligibility for retirement, etc.

1.4 Seek information from industry associations, publications, and state and local government employment offices on the anticipated types and skill levels, over the next few years, of the workers from whom the organization recruits its employees.

1.5 Contact those who contribute to strategic planning to learn if workforce skills analyses are planned or under way. Review the analyses to see if detailed assessments of skills levels are included.

1.6 Regularly contribute to analyses of the organization's present and future workforce skills requirements and the availability of needed skills in the current and projected workforce.

1.7 Participate as a working member in the entire strategic planning process.

2. *Indicator:* HRD programs are endorsed by management as supporting the strategic plan.

Key Steps

2.1 Do an internal review of training programs that have regularly been provided to the organization to assess the extent to which each program addresses strategic priorities of the organization.

2.2 Develop (a) proposed revisions in major programs to align them better with strategic priorities; (b) possible cuts in other programs that don't address strategic priorities, to shift resources to higher priorities; (c) new programs in strategic areas not covered.

2.3 Identify an advisory committee of senior managers, including planners, who review existing and proposed HRD programs to ensure their alignment with the organization's strategic priorities.

2.4 Seek ongoing support from the advisory committee for significant HRD funding as a strategic asset to the organization.

3. *Indicator:* The trainer shares key performance improvement decisions with managers.

Key Steps

3.1 Develop expertise in the seven key performance-related decisions.

3.2 Propose to use the key performance-related decisions with a manager who has a keen interest in a particular performance problem.

3.3 Evaluate the effectiveness of use of the key performance-related decisions and calculate productivity improvements, cost, or time savings.

3.4 Present productivity gains and cost savings from the initial project to top management, and encourage other managers to join in performance improvement projects.

EXPERT HRD RESOURCE

4. *Indicator:* The trainer is recognized as an HRD expert.

Key Steps

4.1 Review models of HRD competencies, select one that fits the organization's HRD approach, and prepare career development plans and individual development plans for all members of the HRD staff.

4.2 Review research on an effective HRD function and analyze its application to the organization.

4.3 Apply new HRD knowledge and skills to one or more existing HRD programs; plan revisions, if appropriate, to improve effectiveness.

4.4 Gain support for program improvements from managers with an interest in those programs; pilot-test the revised programs, evaluate to determine increased effectiveness, and calculate any productivity gains or cost savings.

4.5 Encourage managers across the organization to contact the HRD staff for assistance in solving specific performance problems and in identifying effective outside training resources for their employees.

5. *Indicator:* The trainer provides consulting skills for high-level organizational change efforts.

Key Steps

5.1 Select a consulting skills model and prepare staff development plans.

5.2 Gain experience observing, participating in, and finally leading consulting projects for the organization.

5.3 Serve as a consultant to support high-level strategic change efforts in the organization.

MANAGER OF TRANSFER OF TRAINING

6. *Indicator:* Managers, trainers, and trainees form an effective Transfer Partnership for each HRD program.

Key Steps

6.1 Identify an influential manager with a strong interest in a major HRD program (usually a supervisor of trainees or higher-level manager); provide a briefing on basic transfer concepts: waste of HRD investments resulting from lack of transfer, barriers, transfer strategies, impact of the manager, and the Transfer Partnership.

6.2 Request the influential manager's participation as a "charter member" of the Transfer Partnership who will actively encourage participation by other key managers (all supervisors of trainees and other managers who provide resources—funds, facilities, etc.).

(Cont.)

Figure 10.2 *(Cont.)*

6.3 Work with the charter member to identify other key managers and to select potentially useful transfer strategies that fit the organization's situation and culture—by managers, trainers, and trainees before, during, and after training—from the strategies in Chapters 5 through 8 and summarized in Appendix A.

6.4 In a joint presentation with the charter member, brief the key managers on basic concepts related to transfer (see Step 6.1) and obtain their agreement to participate in the Transfer Partnership and to encourage participation by their trainees.

6.5 Assist the managers in selecting the transfer strategies they agree to use and in planning how to implement them.

6.6 Arrange a meeting with participating managers and trainees to brief trainees on basic transfer concepts, present transfer strategies the managers and trainers will use, help trainees select appropriate transfer strategies for themselves, and plan how to implement them.

7. *Indicator:* The trainer is recognized as manager of transfer for the organization.

Key Steps

7.1 For each major training program, develop baseline data (if possible) on the level of transfer of new skills and the length of time it took to achieve acceptable levels of transfer for previous presentations before the Transfer Partnership was developed.

7.2 Schedule and coordinate all planned transfer strategies by all partners for the next program presentation.

7.3 Prompt and monitor the use of transfer strategies by all three partners (managers, trainers, and trainees) before and during training to ensure timely and effective implementation.

7.4 Bring all Transfer Partnership members together toward the end of the training program to evaluate the effectiveness of transfer strategies used so far and to review the remaining strategies to be used by all partners for this program.

7.5 During the two months or so following the end of formal training, maintain contact with managers and trainees to prompt and monitor the use of the remaining transfer strategies.

7.6 Depending on the nature of the program, bring all Transfer Partnership members together one or more times after the end of training to discuss how well trainees have been able to transfer the training, evaluate the effectiveness of all strategies used, identify barriers that are still interfering with transfer, and develop additional transfer strategies if necessary.

7.7 For each major training program, document the transfer strategies that were used for each presentation by all partners during all time frames and summarize the evaluations of effectiveness of the strategies by all partners.

7.8 For each major program presentation after the Transfer Partnership was initiated, calculate the levels of transfer of new skills and the length of time to reach acceptable levels of transfer; compare these with the baseline data before the use of transfer strategies.

7.9 Get concurrence on these calculations from the other partners and present the results to top management as accomplishments of the Transfer Partnership.

STEPS TO MOVE INTO NEW ROLES

Each organizational situation is different. The steps listed in Figure 10.2 should be considered a flexible guideline; trainers must be alert to opportunities to move on indicators and steps in a different sequence. Also, several steps apply to more than one indicator. For example, applying the performance analysis process (Indicator 3) is one way to demonstrate expertise in HRD (Indicator 4). We see these overlaps as adding to the value of the indicators.

Also, we want to warn you that the hypothetical scenario we use to illustrate the indicators and steps will seem very optimistic. Pat and the HRD staff at Bestway seem to do everything right. The managers and trainees they work with are uniformly supportive and raise no difficult questions or challenges.

We present this rosy scenario as a vision of what might be, a goal toward which to move. We know that real life is never this easy. However, transfer efforts have had an amazingly unifying effect in organizations that have addressed these problems in an orderly fashion based on analysis, good planning, and flexible responses to opportunities. We believe that those of you who follow these steps will be successful in moving into the roles of strategic resource, expert HRD resource, and manager of transfer for your organizations.

STRATEGIC RESOURCE

1. *The trainer participates in the strategic planning process.*

Getting Started

Pat, head of Bestway's HRD function, gathers all possible information about Bestway's strategic planning process: who is involved (particularly in Pat's chain of command), procedures, strategic goals, other reports, current or projected activities, types and sources of information used, and so on. Pat asks the HRD staff to learn all about Bestway's products, services, problems, accomplishments, suppliers, customers, and priorities and to stay informed.

Pat reads *Workforce 2000*, the landmark study of the present and future U.S. workforce through the year 2000. The staff looks for organizational and industry workforce analyses that provide data relevant to Bestway: skill requirements, present and future; availability of needed skills in the current and projected workforce in the coming years; and predicted workforce demographics (education/skill levels, gender, ethnicity, culture, etc.). They contact ASTD's Information Center for help. Through an information search at a local college library, they obtain information from the

ERIC Clearinghouse on Adult, Career, and Vocational Education and from the U.S. Departments of Education and Labor.

Pat and the staff also begin to read HRD professional journals and *The Wall Street Journal*. They develop an internal library of Bestway annual reports and other company studies; industry association publications; local, state, and regional employment studies; and the HRD professional journals.

Pat finds that Bestway has been doing strategic planning for several years. However, the plans do not include detailed workforce projections on demographics of Bestway's—or the industry's—current or future workforce.

Moving Forward

Pat talks to the director of human resources, who contributes directly to the strategic planning process. There are two purposes for this discussion. First, Pat wants to hear about the planning process from someone involved: its successes, shortcomings, future activities, and so on. Second, Pat wants to show that the training function can make an important contribution to the process.

Pat learns that analyses of Bestway's workforce are planned and offers to contribute the industry and workforce analyses the HRD staff has collected. The HRD staff will also help to apply these analyses to Bestway's situation.

Doing Well

Pat is now a respected participant and contributor to Bestway's strategic planning process. The HRD staff participates in regular analyses of present and projected workforce skill requirements and current and projected skill levels for Bestway and the industry. Because workforce skills are seen as directly affecting productivity and competitiveness, these analyses are the basis for important strategic decisions by Bestway top managers on priorities and goals. Pat participates in the decision-making process.

2. HRD programs are endorsed by management as supporting the strategic plan.

Getting Started

Pat begins an internal review of training, education, and career development programs. Several are clearly focused on Bestway's major strategic objectives. Others seem only indirectly related. The HRD staff develops proposed revisions in the first category to eliminate segments that don't have strategic relevance and to strengthen relevant segments. The staff proposes cuts in indirectly related programs (though some are very popular). Finally, they propose development of two new programs that they believe will address strategic priorities they had not previously recognized as important.

Pat's boss tentatively approves the changes and accepts Pat's recommendation to request approval for the revisions by higher management. This would begin the process of shared decision making by Bestway managers and trainers, which Pat sees as essential to link HRD efforts closely to the organization's strategic priorities.

Moving Forward

Pat requests a formal review of recommended changes in HRD programs by those who have been involved in Bestway's strategic planning process and by top managers from major departments. Pat recognizes that this is a calculated risk but decides to gamble on being proactive.

Members of the HRD staff present the results of research on workforce projections and recommend changes in HRD programs to meet strategic objectives. These include performance-related initiatives (e.g., feedback and reward systems) that have not previously been considered HRD activities. The HRD function gains the respect of the planners and top managers, who are impressed by the presentation; the risk pays off. As an added benefit, the managers and planners agree to form an advisory committee to help the HRD function continue to focus on Bestway's strategic goals. They also agree to serve as HRD advocates if budget cuts are proposed.

The HRD staff determines that Bestway currently spends 1.5% of payroll for all HRD programs (job-related training, educational tuition reimbursement, career development, and other performance support projects). They set a goal of 2% and begin research to identify average HRD spending in the industry.

Doing Well

Bestway's HRD advisory committee meets regularly to review current and planned programs and to suggest new requirements and priorities. The HRD staff prepares carefully for these meetings, documenting how HRD programs address strategic priorities and presenting evaluations of employee accomplishments on the job resulting from those programs. The committee continues to support changes to align HRD programs more directly with Bestway's priorities and to support the resulting programs against budget-cutting proposals.

3. The trainer shares key performance improvement decisions with managers.

Getting Started

Pat reviews the key performance improvement decisions (Chapter 3), and obtains copies of the references by Gilbert, Harless, and Mager and Pipe, which give detailed guidance on the performance analysis process. As a learning experience, the HRD staff applies the key performance improvement decisions retroactively to a major training program that the HRD staff developed some years ago. Pat and the staff explore the important considerations for those key decisions using available information.

They conclude that there was evidence of a performance problem big enough (in their opinion) to justify the cost of development of the training program to solve it. So they believe the first key decision was properly made.

However, Pat and the staff realize that no one had ever addressed the rest of the key decisions, starting with possible causes of the performance problem other than lack of knowledge or skill. No one on the HRD staff is familiar with the trainees' work environment or with possible motivation or incentive problems. They begin to gather information on these causes informally from employees who attend the training program using questions suggested by the performance analysis references.

They find evidence of both work environment and motivation/incentive problems, as well as information suggesting that lack of knowledge or skill is also a cause of the performance problems. Pat is relieved that the training program appears justified, and suggests exploring possible transfer strategies. Pat also asks the staff to revise the program's design and delivery to focus only on the skill/knowledge lacks that were corroborated. They will continue using participant reactions as evaluations until new methods can be developed.

Moving Forward

Pat contacts a manager who has sent many employees to the training program and who has indicated concerns that some trainees don't perform as well as expected following the program. Pat presents the HRD staff analysis of the key decisions. The manager is very interested in the key decisions and agrees that there was sufficient evidence of an important performance problem that merits attention.

The manager is intrigued with the questions on potential work environment or motivation/incentive problems. She believes these might explain the performance problems that the training has not solved, and agrees to work with Pat to explore those issues.

They look at the data the HRD staff gathered informally by talking with trainees. They also gather data, by observation and interviews with other employees and supervisors, which confirm that there is some interference with the desired performance in the work environment and some motivation and incentive problems. Pat agrees to help the manager develop possible solutions to those problems by following the performance analysis process further, with help from a group of interested employees. Eventually changes are made in work procedures and feedback systems which resolve most of the nontraining performance problems.

The data collected by Pat and the manager also show that untrained employees lack knowledge and skill necessary to perform effectively. They agree that the training program is still justified. However, they decide to make the revisions which the HRD staff proposed: to focus specifically on high-priority knowledge and skill deficiencies. Pat and the manager also identify transfer strategies (by the manager and supervisors, trainers, and trainees before, during, and after training) that will support more effective transfer of new skills to the job.

The training redesign results in cutting several modules that provided training for performance problems for which work environment and motivation/incentive solutions have been found. This reduces the length of training by one day, giving significant savings in direct and indirect training costs.

The HRD staff calculates productivity gains from the revisions in work procedures and feedback systems. They also calculate the savings on reduced training time plus greater transfer of training to the job. Together the productivity gains and savings from streamlined training and improved transfer are impressive. Pat and the manager agree that working together through the key decisions on performance improvement really paid off.

Doing Well

The manager whom Pat assisted, in the organization's first use of shared decisions on performance improvement, joins Pat in making a presentation to top managers about the success of the project. She points out the hidden problems that were discovered which had undermined productivity, and shows cost savings that resulted from the revision of training. She also describes the benefits of using transfer strategies by managers, trainers, and trainees. Pat describes the coordinated Transfer Partnership now in place to continue support for transfer.

Following this joint presentation, Pat and the HRD staff are called by several other managers. The HRD staff has begun to apply the key decisions on performance improvement to two existing major HRD programs and another proposed program. They are excited by the chance to have a real impact on Bestway's strategies and productivity, and continue to look for new performance improvement opportunities.

EXPERT HRD RESOURCE

4. *The trainer is recognized as an HRD expert.*

Getting Started

Pat and the HRD staff review the references provided in Chapter 3 and order several that fit their organizational situation. Much of the information on performance technology, HRD competencies, and an effective HRD function is new to them. (For example, ASTD's *Models for HRD Practice* defines HRD as including training and development, career development, and organization development [OD]. The staff had never before considered OD as part of HRD.)

These publications stimulate Pat to follow through on an earlier decision to join ASTD, read its journal, *Training and Development*, regularly, and also subscribe to *Training, the Magazine of Human Resources Development*; and *Human Resource Development Quarterly*. The HRD staff develops a shared reading process and plans a monthly meeting to discuss applications of key readings to Bestway programs.

Pat soon becomes aware that there is a local chapter of the National Society for Performance and Instruction (NSPI) in the nearby metropolitan area. A visit to several monthly meetings convinces Pat that this organization is also worth joining. NSPI's journal, *Performance and Instruction*, and the *Performance Improvement Quarterly* are added to the staff's reading list.

Moving Forward

Pat and the HRD staff prepare career development plans for the staff based on the competency model and begin individual development plans for each staff member (including Pat). Pat studies the research on an effective HRD function and leads an internal workshop to apply its criteria and standards to the Bestway HRD function. The staff contacts local resources for developing HRD competencies (colleges, universities, vendors, videotape and computer-based training programs) and schedules in-house and off-site training for the staff.

Pat contacts one of the managers on the advisory committee and proposes an overhaul of the manager's most-used program. The manager is reluctant at first because the program has been consistently highly rated by trainees. However, some revisions proposed as a result of the HRD staff's growing expertise make a lot of sense. One of these is the use of job aids to support more accurate performance while reducing time previously required for trainees to learn complex sequences. The manager agrees to provide subject matter experts to assist in developing the job aids, and to provide trainees for pilot-testing the revised program. The job aids get high marks from trainees and their supervisors, and a small but significant cost savings is achieved.

Based on their reading, training, and involvement in professional associations, Pat and the HRD staff begin to incorporate new HRD methods and techniques in many of the programs they are developing and revising for the organization. They also are able to recommend new approaches to resolving work environment problems and motivation/incentive issues that have not been used previously in the organization.

Doing Well

Pat presents the accomplishments of two redesigned HRD programs to the organization's Executive Committee and the chief executive officer. Pat's boss introduces the presentation and emphasizes two points: the cost savings in reduced training time and the development of workforce skills that support the organization's new strategic priorities. As a result of management interest generated by the presentation, Pat now has a schedule of projects for design and redesign of HRD programs that will keep the staff occupied for the next four months. As a precaution, however, Pat builds in some slack time to allow quick response to a few as yet unforeseen priority projects.

5. *The trainer provides consulting skills for high-level organizational change efforts.*

Getting Started

Pat gets a copy of Block's book on consulting skills (see references, Chapter 3), and reads it carefully. The contacts with managers in working through the key performance improvement decisions provide Pat with an opportunity to practice basic consulting skills in a relatively stress-free environment.

Pat realizes that the HRD staff also needs more training and practice in effective consultation skills. They bring in a professor from a nearby business school, who begins coaching sessions on consulting skills. Each HRD professional, including Pat, develops a consulting project for a Bestway component. These projects are reported weekly in the coaching sessions for guidance from the instructor and critique by other staff members on problems and accomplishments. Managers who are the clients for these consulting projects are generally very pleased with project results.

Moving Forward

The projects turn out to have multiple payoffs beyond immediate project objectives. The increased contacts of HRD staff throughout the organization, combined with their growing HRD and consulting expertise, develop a steady stream of inquiries and requests from managers and employees. The staff is able to resolve many of these through the increased effectiveness of existing HRD programs, referring others to effective external sources, so the number of new projects for the HRD staff is maintained at a reasonable level.

To gain greater experience in consulting skills, Pat arranges a temporary informal "internship" with a professional colleague who is doing a pro bono consulting project with a local community organization. Pat spends 10 hours a week assisting the colleague in all phases of the project and discussing the objectives and techniques for each phase. The colleague gives Pat useful feedback on Pat's skills and accomplishments during the project. Pat feels capable of handling small projects at Bestway: helping managers to deal with difficult employees, helping work teams design and carry out planning workshops for team members, and so on.

Pat is contacted by the organization's comptroller, who is planning an Executive Committee retreat. The CEO wants to begin a team-building process with top managers to build greater effectiveness in meeting Bestway's strategic goals. The team-building process will be introduced at the retreat. The comptroller asks Pat to help identify an organization development consultant to guide the CEO and the committee through the team-building process.

Through contacts from professional association meetings, Pat identifies a consultant who is highly recommended for team-building interventions in similar organizations. Pat confers with the consultant and is impressed with his creativity and experience. They work out a proposed design, schedule, and cost estimates for team-building sessions. Pat suggests that the proposal also include Pat's involvement as adjunct trainer throughout the team-building sessions. The comptroller, the Executive Committee, and the CEO sign off on the proposal, with Pat in charge of planning, logistics, and evaluation of the sessions.

After the first retreat session, the CEO thanks Pat for hard work and leadership in supporting an effective team-building experience. Pat's boss suggests adding organization development management to Pat's responsibilities.

Doing Well

During the year, Pat has continued to learn and practice consulting skills and has provided consulting services for the CEO and other top managers. The projects have included a transition session for an incoming manager, a mediation session between another manager and her valued secretary who had threatened to resign, and coaching in interpersonal communications for a manager whose staff had rebelled at what they called "boot camp" management. For each project Pat has followed a carefully designed consulting plan and is pleased at the positive responses from managers.

MANAGER OF TRANSFER OF TRAINING

6. *Managers, trainers, and trainees form an effective Transfer Partnership for each HRD program.*

Getting Started

Pat reviews research on barriers to transfer of training (Chapter 2) and the lists of transfer strategies before, during, and after training (Chapters 5 through 8 and Appendix A). With one of the HRD staff, Pat studies the Transfer Audit for trainers in Appendix C. They identify several trainer strategies before, during, and after training for immediate use by the HRD staff to support transfer of training for a major organizational HRD program.

They review the manager and trainee strategies, identifying several that seem appropriate for the supervisors and managers of trainees in that program and for the trainees themselves—before, during, and after training. They plan to meet with an influential manager who has a special interest in that program and an experienced employee who is an effective cultural role model for many new employees to discuss the possibility of forming a Transfer Partnership for that program before its next presentation.

Moving Forward

Pat and the HRD staff member develop an adaptation of the trainer's Transfer Audit form (Appendix C) for Bestway managers. They include all manager strategies that might have application at Bestway. They meet with the manager who has a special interest in the training program they reviewed. Pat has prepared a short briefing on concepts of transfer of training: wasted HRD investments resulting from lack of transfer, research results, major barriers, the high impact of manager and supervisor strategies in supporting transfer, the Transfer Partnership and use of transfer strategies. The manager agrees that the whole concept makes a lot of sense.

Pat and the HRD staff member tell the manager about the trainer strategies they have identified and describe how these will be implemented before, during, and after the next training presentation. They then lead the manager through the Manager's Transfer Audit. Two manager strategies are already common practice for this program. The manager identifies several additional strategies on the audit which have high potential for application at Bestway; they fit the organization's culture and the training program's design.

Pat gets this manager's commitment to participate as a "charter member" of the Transfer Partnership for this program and to help encourage participation by other managers. Pat and the charter member identify five other managers who send trainees to this program and/or allocate resources (primarily funds and facilities) for the training. Pat and the charter member present transfer concepts to the five managers. They all review the Manager's Transfer Audit and agree on a group of strategies—before, during, and after training—to support transfer for this program. These managers are also supportive, promise to participate in the selected strategies in all three time frames, and agree to encourage participation by their trainees in the Transfer Partnership.

The other members of the Partnership for this program—the trainees for the next presentation—are invited to a special meeting before training begins. All six managers and the experienced employee who is a good role model are also present; several participate in briefing trainees on the importance of the training program, its content, and the impact on how work is performed. The managers also present the transfer strategies they and the trainers will use and promise to meet with trainees during and after the program to provide support and reinforcement for new skills.

At this meeting the experienced employee helps the trainees review a Trainee's Transfer Audit which the HRD staff has prepared, following the trainer audit model in Appendix C. In small groups they discuss how possible trainee strategies might be used. As a whole group they agree on specific trainee strategies to be pilot-tested for the next program presentation. Trainees express genuine satisfaction at being able to contribute to making the training a successful experience.

Doing Well

Pat and the HRD staff have formed four working Transfer Partnerships for the major HRD programs in the organization. The managers and trainees in each partnership work with the trainer to identify and implement useful transfer strategies. Transfer Partnership members agree that a new set of prospective trainees will be brought in as partnership members for the next presentation of the program. The previous trainee partners will "graduate" to their regular status as employees. However, many welcome the opportunity to serve in a Transfer Partnership for the next HRD program they attend.

7. The trainer is recognized as manager of transfer for the organization.

Getting Started

Pat can find no documentation from previous program presentations indicating the level of transfer after training and the time it took to reach acceptable levels of transfer. Participant reaction sheets, the only data available, simply show high ratings by former participants.

Pat assigns an HRD staff member to record all transfer strategies that have been selected and the dates on which the partnership members will use them. The staff member develops a time chart showing all strategies, who will take the action, and when.

Moving Forward

Pat interviews supervisors of trainees in previous program presentations and gets their estimates of levels of transfer and the time it took following training to reach acceptable performance levels. The transfer strategy chart is then shared with all members of the Transfer Partnership. Before, during, and after training, Pat's staff person reminds all partners of strategies to be used and gets confirmation that they took place. During training, Pat asks all manager partners to join with the trainer and trainees for a brief session to discuss the impact of the strategies to date and to maintain interest and commitment in the strategies to come.

During the period after training, Pat's staff member continues to prompt and monitor use of training strategies. About six weeks after completion of training, Pat calls another meeting of the Transfer Partnership. Most of the managers show up to meet with the trainer and trainees. They review training outcomes and the extent of transfer of training. Overall the level of transfer is definitely higher than the estimates of transfer following previous presentations.

At this meeting they also review the transfer strategies each partnership member took. Most of the transfer strategies were considered useful; some were rated very effective in supporting transfer of the training. A few strategies were considered relatively ineffective, and the partners recommended these be dropped from the next training presentation.

The consensus of managers, trainer, and trainees is that the transfer strategies resulted in an unusually high level of commitment of all partners to the success of the training. Most of the members of the Transfer Partnership—managers, trainers, and trainees—also felt that their cooperative work toward common goals would pay off in greater cooperation in other matters back on the job. Pat is extremely pleased with the outcome of the first full-fledged Transfer Partnership for the organization.

Doing Well

Pat and the HRD staff review what they have learned in managing transfer strategies for these programs. They document the high levels of transfer that now occur regularly for the programs and, with the assistance of Transfer Partnership managers, estimate the resulting increases in productivity.

Pat prepares another briefing for the CEO and the Executive Committee on the success of these four Transfer Partnerships. The briefing presents the productivity gains and the extent to which the organization's investment in training has paid off. Pat is careful to give full credit to the managers and trainees who participated in the partnerships, emphasizing that the support of all is essential in making transfer of training a reality.

The CEO and the board congratulate Pat and the managers, trainers, and trainees who made these Transfer Partnerships successful. The CEO comments that the transfer projects have helped to provide a unified direction for organizational productivity and workforce support programs that is unique in Bestway's history.

DEVELOPING THE TRAINER'S ACTION PLAN: AN OPPORTUNITY FOR RELAPSE PREVENTION

Now let's get back to reality. What will it take for HRD professionals to move toward the successes Pat has accomplished? What should go into your own action plans to move in the same directions? How can we help trainers transfer what they have learned from this book to their organizational situations back on the job?

We suggest that this challenge—to develop an action plan to transfer this learning to the job—is an opportunity to apply the relapse prevention process we described in Chapter 8. Two job aids provided in this book are important resources in developing the plan. First, the summary of steps given earlier in Figure 10.2 provides the basis for the action plan. These seven indicators and 38 steps reflect the experience of many trainers who have formed Transfer Partnerships in many organizations.

Second, the summary of the relapse prevention process, shown in Figure 8.1, gives guidelines for introducing new learning into an organization that is not prepared to support that learning. That may be the situation in your work situations; in many organizations there is little attention to or ready-made support for a unified attack on transfer problems.

We suggest that trainers make copies of Figures 8.1 and 10.2 and compare them. An important next move is to locate the allies mentioned in Step 3 of the relapse prevention process. These might include an interested line manager, a professional colleague in or outside the organization, an eager subordinate, and even a thoughtful trainee. With support from two or three allies, the trainer can work through both sets of guidelines, moving back and forth to apply relapse prevention processes to the seven indicators and 38 steps.

For each indicator, and then for each step, what are predictable problem areas? What coping skills or mechanisms are available? In the trainer's organization, is it better to take steps in a different order? Who are the specific people the trainer should contact, for what purpose, and with what desired outcome?

As the first steps in the trainer's tailored action plan begin to gel, the trainer and allies should plan them in detail. Then they should conduct "fire drills" with allies playing various organizational roles. This allows the trainer to practice the actions and anticipate barriers and difficulties. It is best not to make detailed plans too far into the future; the outcomes of earlier steps will probably require many readjustments to the original plan.

The allies can provide both a feedback mechanism and a cheering section for the trainer who is moving into new territory. Moving into the role of manager of transfer requires ingenuity and effort and poses some risks of rejection and possible failure. However, our experience, and that of many of our colleagues, convinces us that the advantages—new visibility and greater impact for the trainer, and enhanced workforce skills and greater productivity for the organization—make the efforts and risks worthwhile.

SUMMARY

Our goal throughout this book has been to provide information, ideas, concepts, and encouragement for HRD professionals who want to move into new roles in their organizations. We have tried to present these concepts to our readers with some of the excitement and challenge we have felt as we explored the problems and possibilities inherent in transfer of training. We hope you have found valuable ideas here, and we hope equally strongly that our energy and enthusiasm have come across.

The time has come for trainers to demonstrate their professionalism and value to the organizations they serve by becoming respected strategic resources, expert HRD resources, and managers of transfer of training. As the HRD function shows increased payoffs for training investments through enhanced transfer, it will be recognized as a strategic partner by managers at all levels. The ultimate payoff for trainers is the satisfaction and delight they will feel in becoming visible and successful in one of the world's most challenging professions.

References

ERIC (Educational Resource Information Center) Clearinghouse on Adult, Career, and Vocational Education, National Center for Research in Vocational Education, Ohio State University.

Johnston, William B., and Arnold H. Packer. *Workforce 2000.* Indianapolis: Hudson Institute, 1987.

Kearns, David T., Chairman and Chief Executive Officer, Xerox Corporation. Remarks in Accepting ASTD's Award to the Corporation for Excellence in Human Resource Training and Development, Orlando, Florida, May 6, 1990.

U.S. Departments of Education and Labor. *The Bottom Line: Basic Skills in the Workplace.* Washington, D.C.: U.S. Government Printing Office, 1988.

Part IV
APPENDICES

Appendix A

STRATEGIES FOR MANAGING TRANSFER OF TRAINING

Training Stage	Performed by	Action	
Before	Manager	M/B.1	Build transfer of training into supervisory performance standards.
		M/B.2	Collect baseline performance data.
		M/B.3	Involve supervisors and trainees in needs analysis procedures.
		M/B.4	Provide orientations for supervisors.
		M/B.5	Involve trainees in program planning.
		M/B.6	Brief trainees on the importance of the training and on course objectives, content, process, and application to the job.
		M/B.7	Review instructional content and materials.
		M/B.8	Provide supervisory coaching skills.
		M/B.9	Provide time to complete precourse assignments.
		M/B.10	Offer rewards and promotional preference to trainees who demonstrate new behaviors.
		M/B.11	Select trainees carefully.
		M/B.12	Arrange conferences with prior trainees.
		M/B.13	Send co-workers to training together.
		M/B.14	Provide a positive training environment (timing, location, facilities).
		M/B.15	Plan to participate in training sessions.
		M/B.16	Encourage trainee attendance at all sessions.
		M/B.17	Develop a supervisor/trainee contract.
	Trainer	TR/B.1	Align the HRD program with the organization's strategic plan.
		TR/B.2	Involve managers and trainees.
		TR/B.3	Systematically design instruction.
		TR/B.4	Provide practice opportunities.
		TR/B.5	Develop trainee readiness.
		TR/B.6	Design a peer coaching component for the program and its follow-up activities.
	Trainee	TE/B.1	Provide input into program planning.
		TE/B.2	Actively explore training options.
		TE/B.3	Participate in advance activities.
During	Manager	M/D.1	Prevent interruptions.
		M/D.2	Transfer work assignments to others.
		M/D.3	Communicate supervisory/managerial support for the program.
		M/D.4	Monitor attendance and attention to training.
		M/D.5	Recognize trainee participation.
		M/D.6	Participate in transfer action planning.
		M/D.7	Review information on employees in training.
		M/D.8	Plan assessment of transfer of new skills to the job.

	Trainer	TR/D.1	Develop application-oriented objectives.
		TR/D.2	Manage the unlearning process.
		TR/D.3	Answer the "WIIFM" question.
		TR/D.4	Provide realistic work-related tasks.
		TR/D.5	Provide visualization experiences.
		TR/D.6	Give individualized feedback.
		TR/D.7	Provide job performance aids.
		TR/D.8	Provide "Ideas and Applications" notebooks.
		TR/D.9	Create opportunities for support groups.
		TR/D.10	Help trainees prepare group action plans.
		TR/D.11	Have trainees create individual action plans.
		TR/D.12	Design and conduct relapse prevention sessions. (See Chapter 8)
		TR/D.13	Help trainees negotiate a contract for change with their supervisors.
	Trainee	TE/D.1	Link with a buddy.
		TE/D.2	Maintain an "Ideas and Applications" notebook.
		TE/D.3	Participate actively.
		TE/D.4	Form support groups.
		TE/D.5	Plan for applications.
		TE/D.6	Anticipate relapse.
		TE/D.7	Create behavioral contracts.
Following	Manager	M/F.1	Plan trainees' reentry.
		M/F.2	Psychologically support transfer.
		M/F.3	Provide a "reality check."
		M/F.4	Provide opportunities to practice new skills.
		M/F.5	Have trainees participate in transfer-related decisions.
		M/F.6	Reduce job pressures initially.
		M/F.7	Debrief the trainer.
		M/F.8	Give positive reinforcement.
		M/F.9	Provide role models.
		M/F.10	Schedule trainee briefings for co-workers.
		M/F.11	Set mutual expectations for improvement.
		M/F.12	Arrange practice (refresher) sessions.
		M/F.13	Provide and support the use of job aids.
		M/F.14	Support trainee reunions.
		M/F.15	Publicize successes.
		M/F.16	Give promotional preference.
	Trainer	TR/F.1	Apply the Pygmalion Effect.
		TR/F.2	Provide follow-up support.
		TR/F.3	Conduct evaluation surveys and provide feedback.
		TR/F.4	Develop and administer recognition systems.
		TR/F.5	Provide refresher/problem-solving sessions.
	Trainee	TE/F.1	Practice self-management.
		TE/F.2	Review training content and learned skills.
		TE/F.3	Develop a mentoring relationship.
		TE/F.4	Maintain contact with training buddies.

Appendix B

BEHAVIORAL PROCESSES UNDERLYING SUCCESSFUL TRANSFER OF TRAINING

We are singularly focused on the bottom-line results of training. In other words, we are concerned about whether trained employees are more likely to apply effectively what they have learned—especially after all significant barriers have been removed. We suggest, then, that organizational managers still need to understand the process of motivating employees to use what they know.

Managers of transfer need to know the answer to this question: *What are the fundamental and underlying behavioral processes in use in transfer management that help to make it work?* In short, when the HRD professional assumes the role of transfer manager, what relevant behavioral processes can be put to work—by manager or trainer—to produce the desired outcomes? Seven common practices immediately emerge. Understanding of these is important because the HRD professional, as manager of transfer for the organization, must be able to explain and demonstrate these processes to managers and encourage them to use each as appropriate.

POSITIVE EXPECTATIONS

Every major motivational speaker advocates the use of some form of positive self-expectancy to drive oneself to success. Examples include, "I will form good habits and become their slaves" and "Expect the best of yourself and of others too." These approaches build on the idea of the self-fulfilling prophecy, in which the creation of a strong image of success within our (and others') mind(s) helps to guide our behavior (and direct the support from others) toward the achievement of our goals. Thus the first behavioral process at work in transfer management is the creation of a strong commitment to using what was learned through self-talk messages that repetitively state both "I *can* do it" and "I *will* do it." In effect trainers and managers help trainees to visualize successful performance.

CUES

Often trainees know what to do and want to perform but are still reluctant to actually use their new knowledge and skills. In this case the manager's job is to stimulate the desired behavior on the job. This can be as easy as verbally requesting it or reminding trainees to use the newly acquired skills. Often all that is needed is a simple cue (a sign, request, or gentle nudge) to bring the previous learning to the surface.

MODELING

Much attention in recent years has focused on the process of *vicarious learning,* in which trainees learn through observation of, discussions with, or reading examples of other individuals who have applied the learning. Trainees may simply need a role model to show them how the task should be done, as well as to legitimate their right to experiment with the new approach. Further, seeing another person attempt to model the behavior may help to overcome one's fear of failure through learning that it is indeed possible to perform the task. Managers are the most powerful (and available) role models because of the reward, expertise, and referent power they possess in conjunction with their accessibility to the employee. Trainers can also be effective role models, though usually with less impact than the manager simply because of their more limited availability.

GOAL SETTING

Of all motivational theories, goal setting has the widest support from the empirical research literature. Goal theory suggests that employees are more likely to apply new knowledge and skills if they have committed themselves to do so—especially to some significant other (e.g., their manager) in their lives. It is important that the employees' goals be participatively set, specific, challenging, yet achievable.

FEEDBACK

Knowledge of results is an essential prerequisite to lasting behavioral change. Feedback, whether internally generated or from one's supervisor, peers, or the job itself, is a powerful force that encourages continued effort and corrects errors. Feedback is most effective for motivating behavioral change when it is solicited, specific, constructive, timely, and provided by a respected person. Again, the manager is the most powerful regular source of feedback under most conditions.

REINFORCEMENT

It has often been said that "the things that get rewarded get done first." Very few employees will continue an activity that does not provide either extrinsic or intrinsic rewards sooner or later. When demonstrated improvements occur, employees require positive reinforcement (the systematic application of desired rewards contingent on a specified behavior). In short, positive reinforcement is a powerful but often neglected tool for sustaining behavioral change. Frequently the most positive potential source of positive reinforcement is the manager.

PEER PRESSURE/SUPPORT

Trainees are usually social animals; they value group acceptance and often respond well to pressures provided by valued colleagues. This suggests that employees should be trained in natural groups whenever possible. Further, trainees should later be provided with frequent opportunities to meet, share success stories, and solve problems of mutual interest. In this way the natural motivational force of peer pressure can become a supportive element encouraging trainees to apply what they have learned.

At the risk of oversimplifying, we suggest that these seven processes—positive expectations, cues, role models, goal setting, feedback, positive reinforcement, and peer pressure/support—hold some extremely valuable lessons for those interested in understanding *why* transfer management works. We urge you not to neglect them.

Appendix C
THE TRANSFER AUDIT PROCESS

It would be easy for some readers to scan this book, examine the guidelines for facilitating transfer of training summarized in Appendix A, and self-assuredly pronounce, "I'm *already* doing most of what the authors recommend." We sincerely hope that such a self-assessment is accurate, for our dream is for every organization to be doing its utmost to achieve the highest level of financial return on its investments in HRD.

We fear, however, that complacency sometimes underlies such a superficial assessment of "We're doing well." Throughout this book we have argued (not that *all* companies are doing a poor job of aiding the transfer process) only that there is often room for improvement in an organization's transfer strategies. Not all companies should be using all of the transfer actions described in Chapters 5–8 (as summarized in Appendix A). We have only suggested that firms should not be content with the status quo if there is legitimate room for improvement and if the technology for such change exists. This book has presented a comprehensive collection of practical and organizationally tested suggestions for improving organizational practices in the transfer-of-training domain.

You may ask, then, "What *should* we do about transfer of training in our company?" In response, we strongly urge that you first conduct a formal or informal "transfer audit" within your organization. This audit is designed to answer these (and other) questions:

- Which of the several dozen transfer strategies are now being used most extensively?

- Which transfer actions do the respondents believe have the *greatest potential* for application?

- During which *time period* (before, during, or following training) should I most logically intervene with new transfer actions to obtain the greatest payoff from my efforts?

- Which group (trainer, trainees, or manager/organization) is most *underutilized* at the present time?

175

- How do *perceptions* of current and potential transfer management differ across my respondent groups?

The transfer audit process can be used at one or more levels. At the simplest (fastest, cheapest, and least controversial) level is the Trainer Audit. The HRD professional would respond to an audit form similar to that included at the end of this appendix. The trainer begins by reviewing the full list of transfer strategies (see Appendix A), then indicates on the six-point response scales for each strategy a perception of the *current* level of support for that activity (e.g., "To what degree is this action now engaged in?"). This would be followed by an assessment of the perceived *potential* for support (e.g., "To what degree is it possible that this action could be used in my firm?"). The HRD specialist might even wish to prepare and complete three separate forms, assessing the items under control of the manager/organization, trainer, and trainees.

Alternatively, one or more sample groups could be polled for their perceptions of transfer activity in the organization. For example, 50 recent trainees could be sent a similar form listing trainee-oriented transfer actions; the 19 full- and part-time trainers in the organization could complete the trainer-oriented form; and a sample of midlevel managers could be asked to return a third form detailing supervisory/organizational actions. In addition, each group could be given the opportunity to complete one or both of the other forms to allow comparisons of perceptions.

Once the data are tabulated (average "current" and average "potential" scores computed for each item for each respondent group), the transfer strategies with the highest *difference scores* ("potential" score minus the "current" score for a trainer-oriented item) can be listed in rank order. Arrayed in descending order of differences, the first item represents that group's perception of the tactic with the *greatest potential net gain* (over current use), then the second item, and on down the list. The three rank-ordered lists of difference scores for manager, trainer, and trainee can then be used to generate a systematic set of high-potency strategies designed to facilitate transfer of training in the organization. All that remains is implementation of the selected items.

Later—for example, one year following implementation of a transfer management system—the organization should again audit its transfer practices to identify which actions are now perceived to be in use and which still hold the highest potential for further payoff. In this way the audits provide an ongoing series of pictures of the state of affairs regarding transfer actions.

Figure C.1   SAMPLE TRANSFER AUDIT FORM

Assessment by the Trainer of Transfer Strategies

DIRECTIONS: Consider the transfer-related roles you usually play as a trainer. Read carefully each of the following transfer-related actions that are basically under your control. Assess each on a scale of 0-5 (e.g., 0 = extremely low; 5 = very high) with regard to two separate dimensions:

- In column 1, indicate your assessment of the CURRENT level of that activity you believe you engage in regularly. Circle that number.

- In column 2, indicate your assessment of the POTENTIAL level of that activity you believe you could engage in. Circle that number.

Trainer-Related Transfer Strategies	Current Level	Potential Level
A. BEFORE TRAINING, I:		
1. Align the HRD program with the organization's strategic plan.	0 1 2 3 4 5	0 1 2 3 4 5
2. Involve managers and trainees.	0 1 2 3 4 5	0 1 2 3 4 5
3. Systematically design instruction.	0 1 2 3 4 5	0 1 2 3 4 5
4. Provide practice opportunities.	0 1 2 3 4 5	0 1 2 3 4 5
5. Develop trainee readiness.	0 1 2 3 4 5	0 1 2 3 4 5
B. DURING TRAINING, I:		
1. Develop application-oriented objectives.	0 1 2 3 4 5	0 1 2 3 4 5
2. Manage the unlearning process.	0 1 2 3 4 5	0 1 2 3 4 5
3. Answer the "WIIFM?" question.	0 1 2 3 4 5	0 1 2 3 4 5
4. Provide realistic work-related tasks.	0 1 2 3 4 5	0 1 2 3 4 5
5. Provide visualization experiences.	0 1 2 3 4 5	0 1 2 3 4 5
6. Give individualized feedback.	0 1 2 3 4 5	0 1 2 3 4 5
7. Provide job performance aids.	0 1 2 3 4 5	0 1 2 3 4 5
8. Provide "Ideas and Applications Notebooks."	0 1 2 3 4 5	0 1 2 3 4 5
9. Create opportunities for support groups.	0 1 2 3 4 5	0 1 2 3 4 5

(Cont.)

Figure C.1 *(Cont.)*

10. Help trainees prepare group action plans.	0 1 2 3 4 5	0 1 2 3 4 5
11. Have trainees create individual action plans.	0 1 2 3 4 5	0 1 2 3 4 5
12. Design and conduct relapse prevention plans.	0 1 2 3 4 5	0 1 2 3 4 5
13. Help trainees negotiate a contract for change.	0 1 2 3 4 5	0 1 2 3 4 5

FOLLOWING TRAINING, I:

1. Apply the Pygmalion Effect.	0 1 2 3 4 5	0 1 2 3 4 5
2. Provide follow-up support.	0 1 2 3 4 5	0 1 2 3 4 5
3. Conduct evaluation surveys & provide information.	0 1 2 3 4 5	0 1 2 3 4 5
4. Develop and administer recognition systems.	0 1 2 3 4 5	0 1 2 3 4 5
5. Provide refresher/problem-solving sessions.	0 1 2 3 4 5	0 1 2 3 4 5

Appendix D

GLOSSARY

APPLICATION-ORIENTED OBJECTIVES—behavioral statements of what trainees should do once they return to their jobs

BARRIERS TO TRANSFER—the set of actual and perceived factors that inhibit the success of training and development efforts and act as impediments to transfer of training

BASELINE PERFORMANCE DATA—information gathered before training begins which serves at least two functions: identification of training needs and a basis for comparison with posttraining data

BEHAVIORAL CONTRACTING—the process of establishing a strong agreement between two parties in which one specifies his/her desired performance changes and intentions to achieve them, and the other commits to providing certain supportive resources and consequences for those changes

BEHAVIORAL TRANSFER INTENTIONS—trainees' resolutions or commitments to apply some key concepts or skills that they learned during training (a form of visualization)

BENCHMARKING—the process of identifying exceptionally successful practices in use by other individuals, units, or organizations and using those ideas to upgrade one's own practices

CHANGE—the second phase in Lewin's three-stage process, in which the existing equilibrium is disrupted by bringing about a favorable imbalance between driving forces and restraining forces

CRITICAL MASS—the proportion of individuals in an organization (or unit) that is necessary to be trained and/or change their behavior before other (less receptive or less aware) individuals will perceive it to be advantageous to do the same

CUEING—provision of stimuli (through questions, expectations, assertions, etc.) to trainees (a) suggesting that the training to be received will be relevant and useful, and/or (b) evoking recall and usage of training received

DEVELOPMENT—learning activities designed to prepare an employee for future responsibilities in the organization

EDUCATION—learning activities designed to improve the competence of an employee in a specific direction beyond the current job

FAR TRANSFER—the extent to which the trainees apply the training to novel or different situations from the ones in which they were trained

FEEDBACK—the systematic and constructive provision of performance-related information to trainees on the quantity and quality of their use of newly gained knowledge and skills

FEEDFORWARD GUIDANCE—information presented by trainers or managers to trainees which explains what to do to improve performance on the job

FORCE FIELD ANALYSIS—Lewin's process of analyzing the factors working for (driving forces) and against (restraining forces) change to understand in which direction the equilibrium will be adjusted

HUMAN RESOURCE DEVELOPMENT (HRD)—the profession that helps organizations to enhance workforce effectiveness and productivity through learning and other performance improvement activities

HRD CONSULTANT—the professional who serves as a partner with management to link HRD efforts to the organization's strategic direction, to make effective performance-related decisions, and to support constructive organizational change

IDENTICAL ELEMENTS APPROACH—the facilitation of transfer through making the training experience closely similar in nature to the task demands of the job

IMAGING—the process of imprinting in one's mind a mental picture of improved behavior and using that vision to stimulate one's own appropriate behaviors

JOB PERFORMANCE AIDS—any mechanism (e.g., wallet cards, lists, posters, or signs) that cue the performer on when and how to perform the task, thus reducing reliance on memory. Job aids are appropriate when (a) tasks are infrequent and/or complex, (b) there are high negative consequences for error, and/or (c) training to perform the task is expensive

LEARNING COMMUNITY—a group atmosphere in which all participants share responsibility for one another's learning and performance improvement and contribute actively to it

LEVERAGED TRAINING—the incremental gain (e.g., improved performance, payoff) received by the organization from the design, implementation, and use of programs increasing transfer of training

LEWIN'S CHANGE MODEL—a portrait of the modification to any existing social system which flows through three steps from unfreezing to change to refreezing (developed by Kurt Lewin)

MAINTENANCE—the process of continuing to use, and sometimes upgrade, newly acquired knowledge and skills across extended periods

MANAGER—an individual in an organization with authority and responsibility for accomplishing an objective or mission through the efforts of others. Managers range from the chief executive officer (CEO) to the first-line supervisor and team or group leader

MANAGER OF TRANSFER OF TRAINING—the trainer who develops the Transfer Partnership for each high-priority training program, manages all transfer partnerships, and serves as advocate for transfer in the organization

MENTORING PROGRAMS—systems in which experienced and successful employees are matched with newer or junior employees to provide useful job and career guidance and support, as well as advice on mistakes to avoid and skills to develop

NEAR TRANSFER—the extent to which individuals apply what was acquired in training to situations very similar to those in which they were trained

NEGATIVE TRANSFER—situation in which prior learning interferes with the acquisition of new knowledge or skills (also known as *proactive interference*)

NORM OF RECIPROCITY—shared feeling that the provision of a benefit or service by one party in a continuing relationship should be repaid roughly in kind by the other party (useful in buddy systems for mutually supporting transfer)

OVERLEARNING—the practice of encouraging trainees to acquire greater skills than currently needed so as to facilitate the retention and subsequent use of those skills

POSITIVE REINFORCEMENT—the process by which a favorable consequence is systematically provided to a trainee or occurs contingent upon the demonstration of a desirable behavior by the trainee

POSITIVE TRANSFER—a situation in which prior learning assists in acquiring new knowledge or skills (also known as *proactive facilitation*)

PROACTIVE APPROACH—the process of focusing one's efforts on actions that can best be taken *before* an event occurs to bring about the greatest impact

PRINCIPLES APPROACH—the facilitation of transfer to new contexts through presenting general principles and guidelines that have broad applicability

PROPENSITY TO TRANSFER—a measure of trainees' relative inclination to apply the knowledge and skills gained from training; assessment of their commitment or will to change if the opportunity occurs

REALITY CHECK—a reminder by managers or others to trainees that it will not necessarily be easy to apply the new skills learned in the presence of difficulties and obstacles

REFREEZING—the third phase in Lewin's change process, in which new habits are solidified through practice and reinforcement

RELAPSE—the regression to a prior pattern of (less desirable) behavior despite having been trained to perform differently; allowing a single "slip" to become the first step into a series of lapses

RELAPSE PREVENTION—a process by which trainees are helped (during a module incorporated into the training program) to plan for needed support and to practice overcoming difficulties in applying new knowledge and skills in an unsupportive work environment (articulated in HRD literature by Robert Marx)

RETENTION—the degree to which newly acquired knowledge and skills are remembered by the trainee following a learning experience

ROLE MODELING—providing a positive illustration of desirable behaviors for others to observe and imitate

ROLE PLAYERS—the key people potentially involved in bringing about successful transfer of training; typically the trainee, trainee's supervisor, trainer, and other organizational members (higher management, peers, and subordinates)

SELF-FULFILLING PROPHECY—direct or indirect communication of a mental expectation regarding the probability of a future behavior, thus increasing its likelihood (also called the *Pygmalion Effect*)

SELF-MANAGEMENT—the process of assessing variables in one's environment, setting one's own goals, initiating behavior changes, applying new learning, monitoring one's actions, and sustaining one's efforts through self-application of relevant rewards

SKILL PERISHABILITY—the length of time it takes a skill to decline below competency level after it has been initially learned

SOCIAL LEARNING—the process by which trainees acquire skills through the vicarious process of observing others

SOCIAL REINFORCEMENT—any positive publicity, formal or informal, provided to trainees that solidifies their new behaviors

STRATEGIC PLANNING—a formal organizational process that develops a shared set of beliefs about the organization's future and goals and identifies the functions, priorities, and resources that are necessary to reach those goals

SUPPORT GROUPS—collections of two or more individuals with similar needs who meet periodically to discuss current problems and ways to solve them

TEACHABLE MOMENT—a brief and often unplanned period in which trainees are especially receptive to formal or informal training because they sense and accept their own learning needs

TRAINEE—the learner, usually an employee, whose training, education, and development are sponsored by the organization to improve organizational functioning and productivity

TRAINER—an HRD professional, either internal or external to the organization, who analyzes performance problems and designs and delivers, evaluates, manages, and/or supports training in a variety of ways

TRAINING—instructional experiences provided primarily by employers for employees, designed to develop new skills and knowledge that are expected to be applied immediately upon (or within a short time after) arrival on or return to the job

TRANSFER CLIMATE—distinguishing attributes of an organization (or unit) which project to its employees varying degrees of a supportive image conducive to the application of new knowledge and skills

TRANSFER CURVE—a plot of the relationship between the extent of training transferred to the job (usually the vertical axis) and time period (usually the horizontal axis). Preferred patterns are upward-sloping and begin immediately following training

TRANSFER OF TRAINING—the effective and continuing application, by trainees to their jobs, of the knowledge and skills gained in training (both on and off the job). Transfer may encompass both maintenance of behavior and its generalization to new applications

TRANSFER MATRIX—a 3×3 (nine-cell) combination of two dimensions (time and role) useful for classifying both barriers to transfer and transfer-aiding strategies

TRANSFER PARTNERSHIP—the vital cooperation of three key groups—managers (including executives, supervisors, team leaders, etc.) trainers, and trainees—which have a strong interest in a particular training program and have agreed to work together to support the full application of the training to the job

UNFREEZING—the first step in Lewin's three-step change process, in which trainees are encouraged to "let go" of old habits and practices

UNLEARNING—the process of extinguishing or diminishing previous knowledge or skills so as to remove those factors interfering with the learning process

VICARIOUS REINFORCEMENT—the encouragement of retention and use of a new behavior through the trainees' observation of, discussions with, or reading examples of other individuals applying the learning

VISUALIZATION—creating visual images (dominant thoughts) of desired future states and envisioning the satisfactions and/or rewards that would accrue as a result of attaining those states

Appendix E

SELECTED BIBLIOGRAPHY

Adams, J. "Historical Review and Appraisal of Research on the Learning, Retention, and Transfer of Human Motor Skills." *Psychological Bulletin* 101 (1987): 41–74.

Anderson, J. G., and K. N. Wexley. "Applications-Based Management Development." *Personnel Administrator* (November 1983): 39–43.

Atwater, S. K. "Proactive Inhibition and Associative Facilitation as Affected by Degree of Prior Learning." *Journal of Experimental Psychology* (1953): 400–404.

Baldwin, T. T. "The Effect of Negative Models on Learning and Transfer from Behavior Modeling: A Test of Stimulus Variability." *Academy of Management Annual Conference*, New Orleans, La, 1987.

Baldwin, T. T., and J. K. Ford. "Transfer of Training: A Review and Directions for Future Research." *Personnel Psychology* 41 (1988): 63–105.

Baumgartel, H., and F. Jeanpierre. "Applying New Knowledge in the Back-Home Setting: A Study of Indian Managers' Adoptive Efforts." *Journal of Applied Behavioral Science* (November–December 1972): 674–94.

Berke, E. I. "Keeping Newly Trained Supervisors from Going Back to Their Old Ways." *Management Review* (February 1984): 14–16.

Berry, E., and S. Berry. "The Know-It-All Syndrome: What It Is and How to Lick It." *Training* (September 1982): 37–40.

Briggs, G. E. "Transfer of Training." In Bilodeau, ed., *Principles of Skills Acquisition*. New York: Academic Press, 1969.

Broad, M. L. "Management Actions to Support Transfer of Training." *Training and Development Journal* (May 1982): 124–30.

———. "Transfer of Training: Building Manager/Trainer/Trainee Support into the Performance System." In *Performance Technology 1989: Selected Proceedings of the 27th NSPI Conference*. Denver, Colo.: National Society for Performance and Instruction, 1989.

Brown, M. G. "Understanding Transfer of Training." *NSPI Journal* (March 1983): 5–7.

Burke, M. J., R. R. Day. "A Cumulative Study of the Effectiveness of Managerial Training." *Journal of Applied Psychology* 71 (1986): 232–45.

Byham, W. C., D. Adams, and A. Kiggins. "Transfer of Modeling Training to the Job." *Personnel Psychology* 29 (1976): 345–49.

Carver, D. A. "Transfer of Training: A Bibliographic Essay." *Library Administration and Management* (June 1988): 151–53.

Chase, A., and P. Wolfe. "Off to a Good Start in Peer Coaching." *Educational Leadership* 46, no. 8 (1989): 37.

Clark, R. C. "Nine Ways to Make Training Pay Off on the Job." *Training* (November 1986): 83–7.

Clement, R. "Management Development in the 1980's: A Field in Transition." *Journal of Management Development* 7 (1988): 45–55.

Cohen, D. J. "The Pre-Training Environment: An Empirical Investigation of Trainee Motivation." In *Southern Management Association Proceedings*. Atlanta, November 1988.

————. "What Motivates Trainees?" *Training and Development Journal* (November 1990): 91–93.

————. "The Pre-Training Environment: A Conceptualization of How Contextual Factors Influence Participant Motivation." *Human Resource Development Quarterly* (Winter 1990): 387–98.

Cormier, S. *Transfer of Training: An Interpretive Review*. Technical Report no. 608. Alexandria, Va.: Army Research Institute for the Behavioral and Social Sciences, 1984.

Crafts, L. W. "Transfer as Related to Number of Common Elements." *Journal of General Psychology* (1935): 147–58.

Cripple, G. H., and H. E. Litchfield. "How to Prepare Your People." *Training and Development Journal* (August 1981): 20–22.

Diekhoff, G. M. "How to Teach, How to Learn." *Training* (September 1982): 36–40.

Duncan, C. P. "Transfer after Training with Single versus Multiple Tasks." *Journal of Experimental Psychology* (1958): 63–72.

Eden, D., and G. Ravid. "Pygmalion versus Self-Expectancy: Effects of Instructor- and Self-Expectancy on Trainee Performance." *Organizational Behavior and Human Performance* (1982): 351–64.

Ehrenberg, L. M. "How to Ensure Better Transfer of Learning." *Training and Development Journal* (February 1983): 81–83.

Ellis, H. D. *The Transfer of Learning*. New York: Macmillan, 1965.

Feldman, M. "Successful Post-Training Skill Application." *Training and Development Journal* (September 1981): 72–75.

Finn, W. T. "Keep Your Eye on the Sales Training Manager." *Training and Development Journal* (July 1984): 65–67.

Fleming, R. K. "Participatory Tactics to Promote Transfer of Training." *49th Academy of Management Conference*, Washington, D.C., August 1989.

————. "A Behavioral Approach to Transfer of Leadership Skills." *Organizational Behavior Teaching Review* (forthcoming).

Ford, J. K. "Understanding Training Transfer: The Water Remains Murky." *Human Resource Development Quarterly* (Fall 1990): 225–29.

Forgus, R. H., and R. J. Schwartz. "Efficient Retention and Transfer as Affected by Learning Method." *Journal of Psychology* (1957): 135–39.

Foxon, M. "Transfer of Training—A Practical Application." *Journal of European Industrial Training* 11, no. 3 (1987): 17–20.

Frank, E., and C. Margerison. "Training Methods and Organization Development." *Journal of European Industrial Training* 2 (1978).

Gagne, R. M., and H. Foster. "Transfer to a Motor Skill from Practice on a Pictured Representation." *Journal of Experimental Psychology* (1949): 342–54.

Gagne, R. M., K Baker, and H. Foster. "On the Relation between Similarity and Transfer of Learning in the Discriminative Motor Tasks." *Psychological Review* (1950): 67–79.

Gall, A. L. "You Can Take the Manager out of the Woods, But . . ." *Training and Development Journal* (March 1987): 54–58.

Garmston, R. J. "How Administrators Support Peer Coaching." *Educational Leadership*, 44, no. 5 (1987): 18–26.

Georgenson, D. L. "The Problem of Transfer Calls for Partnership." *Training and Development Journal* (October 1982): 75–78.

Gist, M. E., A. G. Bavetta, and C. K. Stevens. "The Effectiveness of Self-Management vs. Goal Setting Training in Facilitating Training Transfer." *Academy of Management 1990 Annual Meeting*. San Francisco, August 12–15, 1990.

———. "Transfer Training Method: Its Influence on Skill Generalization, Skill Repetition, and Performance Level." *Personnel Psychology* 43 (Autumn 1990): 501–523.

Goldstein, I. L., and G. A. Musicante. "The Applicability of a Training Transfer Model to Issues Concerning Rater Training." In *Generalizing from Laboratory to Field Settings*, edited by E. Locke, 83–98. Lexington, Mass.: Lexington Books, 1985.

Graham, K. R., and A. A. Vicere. "B.E.O.C. (Big Executives On Campus)." *Training and Development Journal* (June 1984): 28–30.

Haselrud, G. M., and S. Meyers. "The Transfer Value of Given and Individually Derived Principles." *Journal of Educational Psychology* (1958): 293–98.

Hearn, W. M. "Beyond Training: A Process Model for Transfer, Evaluation, and Institutionalization." *Journal of Management Development* 7, no. 3 (1988): 22–28.

Hendrickson, G., and W. Schroeder. "Transfer of Training in Learning to Hit a Submerged Target." *Journal of Educational Psychology* (1941): 206–13.

Hendrickson, J. "Training in Context." *Training* (March 1990): 65–70.

Hicks, W. D., and R. J. Klimoski. "Entry into Training Programs and Its Effects on Training Outcomes: A Field Experiment." *Academy of Management Journal* 30 (1987): 542–52.

Hoffman, F. O. "Training Technology's Next Frontier: On-the-Job Performance Objectives." *Training* (September 1983): 57–59.

Hollingsworth, A. T., and D. T. Hoyer. "How Supervisors Can Shape Behavior." *Personnel Journal* (May 1985): 86–88.

Huczynski, A. A., and J. W. Lewis. "An Empirical Study into the Learning Transfer Process in Management Training." *Journal of Management Studies* (1980): 227–40.

Jamieson, D., and J. O'Mara. *Managing Workforce 2000: Gaining the Diversity Advantage*. San Francisco: Jossey-Bass, 1991.

Kaman, V. S. "Predict Training Fortunes." *Personnel Journal* (May 1985): 42–47.

Kanfer, F. "Self-Management Methods." In *Helping People Change: A Textbook of Methods*, edited by F. H. Kanfer and A. P. Goldstein. 2d ed. New York: Pergamon Press, 1980.

Kelley, A. I., R. F. Orgel, and D. M. Baer. "Seven Strategies that Guarantee Training Transfer." *Training and Development Journal* (November 1985): 78–82.

Kelly, H. B. "A Primer on Transfer of Training." *Training and Development Journal* (November 1982): 102–6.

Kent, R. H. "Transfer of Training without the Boss." *European Journal of Industrial Training* (Spring 1982): 17–19.

Knox, A. B. "Helping Adults Apply What They Learn." *Training and Development Journal* (June 1988): 55–59.

Kruger, M. J. "Two Techniques to Ensure that Training Programs Remain Effective." *Personnel Journal* (October 1985): 70–75.

Kruger, M. J., and G. D. May. "Transfer of Learning in Management Training: Building the Payoff into the Instructional Design." *Performance and Instruction Journal* (April 1986): 3–6.

Laker, D. R. "Dual Dimensionality of Training Transfer." *Human Resource Development Quarterly* 1 (1990): 209–23.

———. "Yes, the Water Remains Murky: But It Is Safe to Swim." *Human Resource Development Quarterly* 1 (1990): 231–35.

Latham, G. P., and C. Frayne. "Self-Management Training for Increasing Job Attendance: A Followup and a Replication." *Journal of Applied Psychology* 74 (1989): 411–16.

Latham, G. P., and L. M. Saari. "Importance of Supportive Relationships in Goal Setting." *Journal of Applied Psychology* (1979): 163–68.

Leifer, M. S., and J. W. Newstrom. "Solving the Transfer of Training Problems." *Training and Development Journal* (August 1980): 42–46.

Lipshitz, R., V. Friedman, and H. Omer. "Overcoming Resistance to Training: A Nonconfrontive Approach." *Training and Development Journal* (December 1989): 46–50.

Lombardo, C. A. "Do the Benefits of Training Justify the Costs?" *Training and Development Journal* (December 1989): 60–64.

Luthans, F., and T. R. V. Davis. "Beyond Modeling: Managing Social Learning Processes in Human Resource Training and Development." *Human Resource Management* (Summer 1981): 19–27.

Mahoney, F. "Targets, Time, and Transfer: Keys to Management Training Impact." *Personnel* 57 (1980): 25–34.

Mandler, G. "Transfer of Training as a Function of Response Overlearning." *Journal of Experimental Psychology* (1954): 411–17.

Manz, C. C., and H. P. Sims, Jr. "Self-Leadership: Developing Skills for Improving and Maintaining Individual Performance." *American Psychological Association Conference*, Toronto, Ontario, August 24–28, 1984.

Marx, R. D. "Relapse Prevention for Managerial Training: A Model for Maintenance of Behavior Change." *Academy of Management Review* (July 1982): 433–41.

———. "Relapse Prevention in Management Training: Self-Control Strategies for Skill Retention." *American Psychological Association Conference*, Toronto, Ontario, August 24–28, 1984.

———. "Self-Managed Skill Retention." *Training and Development Journal* (January 1986): 54–57.

Marx, R. D., and R. J. Karren. "The Effects of Relapse Prevention Training and Post-Training Followup on Time Management Behavior." *Academy of Management 1990 Annual Meeting*, San Francisco, California, August 12–15, 1990.

McCormick, W. "You Can Avoid the Transfer Training Trap." *Sales and Marketing Management* (May 1990): 84–88.

McLagan, P. S. "Top Management Support." *Training* (May 1988): 59–62.

Michalak, D., and E. Yager. *Making the Training Process Work.* New York: Harper & Row, 1979. See especially chapter 7, "Maintenance of Behavior," pp. 119–27.

Mosel, J. N. "Why Training Programs Fail to Carry Over." *Personnel* (1957): 56–64.

Musselwhite, W. C., and L. S. Dillon. "Timing, for Leadership Training, Is Everything." *Personnel Journal* (May 1987): 103–10.

Musselwhite, W. C. "The Impact of Timing on Readiness to Learn and Transfer of Learning from Leadership Development Training: A Case Study." Doctoral dissertation, North Carolina State University, 1985.

Nadler, L. "Support Systems for Training." *Training and Development Journal* (October 1971): 2–7.

Napier, N., and J. Deller. "Train Right or Don't Train at All." *Training and Development Journal* (February 1985): 90–93.

Newstrom, J. W. "A Role-Taker/Time-Differentiated Integration of Transfer Strategies." *American Psychological Association Conference*, Toronto, Ontario, August 24–28, 1984.

———. "A Contingency Model for Addressing the Impediments to Transfer of Training." *Academy of Management National Conference*, San Diego, August 1985.

———. "Leveraging Management Development through the Management of Transfer." *Journal of Management Development*, no. 5 (1986): 33–45.

Noe, R. "Trainees' Attributes and Attitudes: Neglected Influences on Training Effectiveness." *Academy of Management Review* 11 (1986): 736–49.

Noe, R. A., and N. Schmitt. "The Influence of Trainee Attitudes on Training Effectiveness: Test of a Model." *Personnel Psychology* 39 (1986): 497–523.

Noe, R. A., J. Sears, and A. M. Fullenkamp. "Relapse Training: Does It Influence Trainees' Post-Training Behavior and Cognitive Strategies?" *Journal of Business and Psychology* (Spring 1990): 317–28.

Parry, S. "Why Training Fails." *Training World* (May-June 1978): 35–39, 47.

Petrini, Catherine S., ed. "Bringing It Back to Work." *Training and Development Journal* (December 1990): 15–21.

Phillips-Jones, L. "Establishing a Formalized Mentoring Program." *Training and Development Journal* (February 1983): 38–43.

Porter, G. "Transfer-Oriented Training: Pre-Design Activities to Enhance the Transfer Process." *Academy of Management 1990 Annual Meeting*, San Francisco, California, August 12–15, 1990.

Rackham, N. "The Coaching Controversy." *Training and Development Journal* (November 1979): 12–16.

"Reminder Cards Meet Self-Affirmation." *Training* (August 1989): 71–72.

Robinson, D. G., and J. C. Robinson. "Breaking the Barriers to Skill Transfer." *Training and Development Journal* (January 1985): 82–83.

———. *Training for Impact*. San Francisco: Jossey-Bass, 1989.

Robinson, J. C. "You Should Have Sent My Boss." *Training* (March 1984): 45–47.

Royer, J. M. "Theories of Transfer of Learning." *Educational Psychologist* 14 (1979): 53–69.

"Rx for 'Training Fadeout': Feedback, Feedback, and More Feedback." *Training* (February 1984): 16, 70.

Sanders, L. W. "Help Your Subordinates Grow." *Personnel Journal* (January 1984): 66–67.

Schlein, R., and N. Edgerton. "Training: How to Get It out of the Classroom." *Training and Development Journal* (September 1985): 84–86.

Sedlick, J. M., A. K. Magnus, and E. Rakow. "Key Elements to an Effective Training System." *Training and Development Journal* (July 1980): 10–12.

Sims, H. P., Jr., and C. C. Manz. "Modeling Influences on Employee Behavior." *Personnel Journal* (January 1982): 58–65.

Spice, M. B., and S. Kopperl. "Are Your Trainees Willing?" *Training and Development Journal* (May 1984): 30–32.

Spitzer, D. R. "But Will They Use Training on the Job?" *Training* (September 1982): 48, 105.

Sredl, H. J., and W. J. Rothwell. "Transfer of Learning—Key to HRD Success." In *The ASTD Reference Guide to Professional Roles & Competencies*, pt. 11, vol. II, 357–401. Amherst, Mass.: HRD Press, 1987.

Stokes, T. F., and P. G. Osnes. "An Operant Pursuit of Generalization." *Behavior Therapy* 20 (1989): 337–55.

Stroul, N., and G. Schuman. "Action Planning for Workshops." *Training and Development Journal* (July 1983): 41–46.

Trammell, N. C., Jr. "An Examination of the Level of Transfer of Skills and Supervisory Involvement in a Presentation Skills Program." Doctoral dissertation, Vanderbilt University, May 1987.

"Transfer of Training." *Training* (November 1989): 72–75.

Trost, A. "They May Love It but Will They Use It?" *Training and Development Journal* (January 1985): 78–81.

Van Velsor, E. "Can Development Programs Make a Difference?" *Issues and Observations* (November 1984): 1–5.

Van Velsor, E., and W. C. Musselwhite. "The Timing of Training, Learning, and Transfer." *Training and Development Journal* (August 1986): 58–59.

Vandenput, M. "The Transfer of Training." *Journal of European Training* 3 (1973).

Watson, C. E. "Getting Management Training to Pay Off." *Business Horizons* (February 1974): 51–57.

Wexley, K. N., and T. T. Baldwin. "Post-Training Strategies for Facilitating Positive Transfer: An Empirical Exploration." *Academy of Management Journal* (September 1986): 503–20.

Wexley, K. N., and W. Nemeroff. "Effectiveness of Positive Reinforcement and Goal Setting as Methods of Management Development." *Journal of Applied Psychology* (1979): 239–46.

Wise, R. E., and H. R. Zern. "Identifying and Improving Management Skills at Hartford National Bank." *Training* (November 1982): 56–58.

Woodrow, H. "The Effect of Type of Training upon Transference." *Journal of Educational Psychology* (1927): 159–72.

Zemke, R., and J. Gunkler. "28 Techniques for Transforming Training into Performance." *Training* (April 1985): 48–63.

Zenger, J. "The Painful Turnabout in Training." *Training and Development Journal* (December 1980): 36–49.

Zigon, J. "Commentary: Change as a Performance To Be Engineered." In *Introduction to Performance Technology*. Washington, D.C.: National Society for Performance and Instruction, 1986.

Zigon, J., and B. Cicerone. "Teaching Managers How to Improve Employee Performance." *Performance and Instruction Journal* (September 1986): 3–6.

Index